SOCIOPATH

The Ultimate Guide to Sociopathy, Psychopathy, and Narcissism

(Learn How to Deal With a Sociopath and Free Yourself From Emotionally Abusive Relationships!)

Johnny Solares

Published by Harry Barnes

Johnny Solares

Sociopath: The Ultimate Guide to Sociopathy, Psychopathy, and Narcissism (Learn How to Deal With a Sociopath and Free Yourself From Emotionally Abusive Relationships!)

ISBN 978-1-77485-105-0

Legal & Disclaimer

The information contained in this book is not designed to replace or take the place of any form of medicine or professional medical advice. The information in this book has been provided for educational and entertainment purposes only.

The information contained in this book has been compiled from sources deemed reliable, and it is accurate to the best of the Author's knowledge; however, the Author cannot guarantee its accuracy and validity and cannot be held liable for any errors or omissions. Changes are periodically made to this book. You must consult your doctor or get professional

Table of Contents

Introduction

Indeed, being mere constituents of a big and largely populated society, building and maintaining good relationships with other people is one very vital aspect of our lives. And more often than not, it is something which we cannot so easily avoid, unless we deliberately choose to live in a totally secluded place and decidedly go on with our lives with no one else but ourselves.

In general, other people will always play a certain part in our lives. Some individuals may have more significant roles than the others. Some may just briefly pass through our lives while the others may become a huge part of more stable and more permanent relationships.

But all the same, we cannot deny the fact that how we go on with our relationships and how we deal with other individuals we encounter in our society are particular components which may considerably influence the quality of life that we will lead throughout our existence in this planet.

The most important relationships in our lives typically include those with our family members, our romantic partners, friends, and co-workers, among all others. Most of the time, we are able to build genuine and fruitful bonds with people in these relationships and this significantly leads to our lives becoming even more meaningful and worth living.

However, not all people are able to do this and sometimes, the inability to do so is mainly a result of mental conditions which heavily affect personality and consequently, the way individuals behave towards other people. One such condition is a particular mental disorder referred to as sociopathy.

Chapter 1: Identifying The Signs

Understanding the signs and characteristics of a sociopath is incredibly important. However, that being said, be cautious because many of the signs associated with sociopathic behavior can be linked to other personalities as well. One of the first signs to look out for is a large ego. While there's absolutely nothing wrong with having confidence, in fact, it's highly encouraged, a red flag may be raised if an individual has an ego that seems out of the ordinary. Evaluate the ego of the person in question. If they seem as though the world is great because they're in it, well they may just be arrogant, but if that level of arrogance rolls over to an unhealthy level, then this may be a sign of a personality disorder. When someone is a sociopath, they feel as though they rule the world, as if nothing and no one is above them.

The sociopath may fall into different categories, the sociopath may be a thief, a murderer, a child who hurts animals and other children around him, and it may even be the individual you thought was your best friend who it turns out was lying to you for years. There are different types of sociopaths. Some sociopath's characteristics are obviously much more severe than others. One quality that most sociopaths have in common is their image. To a sociopath the way they look and the way they are perceived by others is everything. Along with the way they look, what really makes them stand out amongst the crowd is their charm. Now, this isn't just your ordinary, we just met, amount of charm. The charm that comes from a sociopath is abnormal, however, you will become so incredibly fixated on this charm that you will not think about anything else. In fact, many individuals become romantically involved with a sociopath after their first meeting because of the amount of charm that exudes from the sociopath. There are many examples of this type of charm. The charm can range from many different areas. For example, when you first meet a sociopath, whether it be a man or woman, they will try and flatter you. The sociopath will try and flatter you in many different ways. You may be flattered when he expresses to you how beautiful he thinks you are and that he has never met someone as beautiful and good looking and let's be honest, we all like to receive compliments at times. We are often drawn to individuals who give us compliments because they make us feel good about ourselves.

While these compliments usually start off after the initial meeting, they tend to continue throughout the course of your relationship with this person. You may find this individual giving you compliments when you feel like you don't deserve them or if you feel like they're not true. For example, most women tend to not feel as pretty in the morning when they first wake up, or when we're sick. Well, if you find that the person of interest is constantly telling you how beautiful you are even during times when you don't feel pretty, it may be true but it may just be the sociopath using his charm on you. Pay attention to the way the person of interest expresses what he's saying, if it feels forced or fake, it probably is. Now, keep in mind that our logical self will probably tell us that what they're saying isn't true, however, our ego will tell us that it is. Let's be honest, we all like to receive compliments and we like to be flattered so it's hard to be rational during these times but if you pay attention to the signs. If you pay attention to the signs and you know what to look for with this charming behavior, you'll know whether or not you can truly believe what the person is telling you or if they are just trying to trick you. That being said, the sociopath when not only try and trick and manipulate you, he will try and charm everyone around him into believing his tricks. Most likely, if you feel a certain way about someone, your family and friends will feel the same way too. If you feel like this man is so sweet, charming and perfect, he will probably be able to convince your family to see him the same way as well.

A sociopath is someone that always knows exactly what to say at exactly the right time. This person is so smooth with his words that you have a hard time not believing everything that comes out of his mouth. When he walks into a room, it automatically lights up due to the overwhelming amount of charisma and energy that radiates from this individual. People are not only drawn to him but they want to be friends with him, they want to date him, they may even want nothing more than to be him. Everyone wants attention and that's exactly what a sociopath receives. A sociopath will often be one that has a great deal of followers. For example, Charles Manson, historical cult leader is considered a sociopath due to his charm, energy and his ability to get so many people to follow exactly what he wanted them to do. Manson was a murderer but never actually murdered anyone because he convinced others to do the work for him. Manson had such a way with words that he was able to take completely ordinary people with no history of psychological issues and make them turn into cold blooded killers. This is part of the charm and energy that sociopaths have. What a sociopath says is often never believable, it's almost always a lie, but these lies sound so convincing because of the way this individual relays the information. When a sociopath is discussing something, they are able to fabricate a complete story and make others believe that it's true, the sociopath himself also believes that these stories are true as well. Manson for example was known to have expressed that he never had to kill anyone, he could just think about it and it would happen. These thoughts were most likely conversations that he had with his followers. Thoughts that he embedded into their brains through his charisma and addictive personality. When an individual is as charming as a sociopath, they are able to convince even the most level headed individual that what they are saying is true. Never being stuck for something to talk about or information to spread and never being short of words or boring is an overwhelming quality to have. Most of us have trouble communicating during certain situations or during different times in our lives. This is different for sociopaths as they never lack words and they always have a response, an answer or a solution to whatever they are faced with. If someone questions their honesty, they in turn will be even more charismatic and make the individual who is questioning them actually change their mind and end up trusting what the sociopath is saying after all. This is why it's so difficult to actually convict sociopaths who are murders because so many individuals tend to believe what they say and if they say they didn't commit the crime, people believe them. It's not until someone categorizes these individuals as a sociopath when the truth comes out.

Part of the game that sociopaths play is that they make you believe that they think very highly of you. They make you feel as though you are the best person in the world. They believe in you, they think you are beautiful in every way, they trust you and want you to trust them as well. While these don't necessarily seem like bad qualities to have, no one will think this way about you 100% of the time. The reality is that people will love you, they will respect you, they will care about you and believe in you but things will never be perfect. The sociopath makes you believe that you are perfect and they are able to give you so many compliments that you often start to question why no one else in your life treats you the way that this person does. Why doesn't everyone else in your life love you and care about you the way this person does? Well, that's exactly what the sociopath wants you to do. He is so smooth, cool, calm and collected with his words that he wants you to feel like he loves you and cares about you more than anyone else. He wants you to question the other people in your life that way you're only drawn to him and what he wants from you. This is exactly how cult leaders such as Manson gain their followers. These cult leaders prey on innocent and vulnerable individuals who will believe everything they say. If someone is standing in front of you telling you how they love you more than anyone else, how they'll always be there for you above anyone else, and you're an individual with low self-esteem, you may end up believing every single word they say and ultimately end up following everything they want you to do.

Sociopaths are narcissists, their egos are so huge that they actually believe that they are the greatest thing that has happened to the world. The huge ego that they carry actually helps them attract others. Now, sociopath attract people into their lives by informing others of all the great qualities that they carry. More often than not, these individuals will discuss all of the wonderful things they've done in their lives. These individuals may start to discuss the Ivy League school where they went to school, they may discuss their entrepreneur plan for the future, and maybe they'll even discuss how many wonderful jobs they've had because everyone wants them to work for their company. Sociopaths will often discuss how wanted they are by the opposite sex to make you want them even more, but they will be sure to let you know how special you are and that's why they chose you to have in their lives. These individuals will display an "I'm on top of the world" attitude. They will act as though they are so far up no one can reach them and no one will be able to outdo their greatness. These individuals will then act like it's a privilege for you to be in their lives because of how great they are.

Think of someone who is in sales, maybe someone who is selling furniture or a car sales men. People who are in sales have been trained to have this over the top personality that can be so influential, they can literally sell anything. For example, maybe you're looking for a new car and you head over to the car lot. While you're there you meet a salesman who is trying to sell you a used car. This salesman knows within himself that this car is not a good choice. He knows what's wrong with the car, how many miles it has on it and in reality, what it's really worth. That being said, he wants to make commission, that's his goal, so he finds ways to encourage you to buy the car. This sales man may need to make things up, point out things that aren't true on the car and hide the truth about how many miles are on the car and how much damage has been done to the vehicle. He will make this car, that really isn't in good shape at all, sound so wonderful that you end up buying the car only to find out later that the car is a lemon. Well, had you known this information ahead of time, maybe you wouldn't have bought the car, but then again, maybe you would have. Oftentimes, when individuals have a way with words, they can convince others to do something they wouldn't normally do. While the ability to sell items is great, it's the individual who is trying to sell himself who you really need to watch out for.

Chapter 2: What Causes Sociopathic Behavior?

Although a number of researches give varying findings, most of them agree upon some common factors. For example, it is thought that sociopathy is caused by genetic as well as environmental factors. An individual may be born with a susceptibility to APD. As the person ages, they may undergo certain experiences or treatment that may trigger the disorder. As at now, it is not well known how genetics can contribute to the development of APD.

Diagnosis of a sociopath

There are a number of characteristics that can tell if one is developing the condition. These include:

Egocentrism- An individual tends to love self more than anyone else. They also believe the only way to boost their self-esteem is to have or possess more power. They also enjoy personal pleasure. At the same time, their goals are set based on self-gratification. It does not matter to them if the means for achieving their goals is legal or not.

They lack empathy- Hurting people cannot make them feel guilty.

They do not have true emotional and romantic relationships because in most instances, they exploit their partners through the use of;

Coercion.

Deceit.

Control by intimidation.

Control by dominance.

Show of hostility towards others. This is shown by someone constantly assaulting a partner, friend or even children, irresponsible behavior by not being committed to financial obligations, disregarding promises and agreements, making decisions without thinking, taking risks that are likely to backfire or result in huge damages among others.

Nervousness and agitation. Sociopaths get easily enraged over small disagreements and can fly into fits of anger that can lead to untold injury or damage.

Most sociopaths are uneducated, though a small number have got education. For the partly educated with proper jobs, they are unable to keep them for long periods of time.

Chapter 3: Narcissist Ned

Ned is the type of person who seems to be only interested in himself — he thinks that he is good-looking and all the women he meets are interested in marrying him. He thinks that he is the best person to talk to about anything, and he annoys people because he never seems to be nice without a reason.

You have been into an argument with Ned once, and it went miserably. He made a mistake on a very important report, and as his teammate, you went ahead and told him that he had to correct his error. To your surprise, he said right to your face that there was no error when he last touched that document. "You placed it there and now you're pinning that booboo on me!" he screamed. To make things worse, he started telling everyone that you are hell-bent on bringing him down because you envy his success.

Now that he needs you to do something for him, he acts as if that argument didn't happen — as if he did not go around telling everyone how horrible you were and bad-mouthing you. However, you are quite sure that he would stop being nice once you grant his request. What are you going to do?

Understanding Ned

A person like Ned is called a narcissist because he upholds a malignant sense of self-love. He does not see anything wrong with him at the surface, but it is very likely that he is suffering from a deep-seated sense of insecurity. Most of the time, people like Ned have not come to terms with the reality that perfect does not exist — as well his fear of failure.

What makes Ned a very difficult person to deal with is that you see that he is leaving a trail of pain. His sense of self is so overwhelming that he begins to lack any empathy or sensitivity to the needs of others. Because of his insecurity, he would want to project his mistakes to other people, become controlling, aggressive, or even scheming in order to get what he wants.

However, there are narcissists who are not as grandiose as Ned. While they may still be self-centered, their selfishness manifests in a less obvious way. If you have a friend who always pretends that he is sick in order to get attention and get his needs taken care of by other people, then you have encountered the other type of narcissist.

Gaining Control of the Situation

The best possible way to deal with a person like Ned is to keep your relationship with him, but from a distance. However, if you have to deal with him directly, here are the things that you can do.

1. Don't let your emotions get the best of you.

Narcissists are masters of emotional manipulation — they can be sweet talkers or extra aggressive in order for them to get the upper hand and order you around. Just remember that you do not have to attend to a narcissist's every need in order to keep the peace. You also do not need to succumb to every argument that an aggressive narcissist "invites" you into just to enable himself to project his flaws to you. Keep calm and be mindful of his actions.

2. Consider the context carefully.

Narcissists do not always act the way that you may predict they would — it is not an all-or-nothing condition. Like any behavior, there are situations that trigger a person's narcissism. Now, it is very important to identify where that behavior is coming from. Once you pinpoint where the insecure behavior is coming from, you would know how to avoid it next.

3. Recognize your own feelings and validate them.

There are a lot of times when a narcissist may project their own problems onto you or manipulate you into taking care of their own responsibilities. When you feel that this person's behavior is leading you to doubt yourself or that you are being sweet-talked into doing something that you should not be doing, remind yourself that those thoughts are valid. Draw the line there and do not be afraid to say no.

Chapter 4: How To Spot A Sociopath?

As already mentioned, spotting a sociopath may be like looking for a needle in a hay stack. Not that they are small in number – 4% of the general population can be termed as sociopaths. The problem arises when you may look at everyone suspiciously trying to evaluate their status as a probable sociopath. We are as much different psychologically as we are physically. Each one of us is unique. Some may have some quirky lifestyle which may be mistaken as sociopathic. People can behave differently without begetting the label of a sociopath. So, what sets sociopaths apart from others whom we consider normal? How to spot one?

Sociopaths never learn, in the sense that normal human beings test the limits of law but remain within its boundaries. You may tell small lies, go late for work and take a long time at the water cooler. These are attempts to subvert the law in a small way, but when a person breaks the law by intentionally driving in a drunken state, knowing fully well that they may cause a fatal accident, they cross the boundary. Sociopaths land in trouble because of their scant regard for social taboos and laws.

You should not mistake introvert as a sociopath. An introvert is simply a shy being who does not have the traits to engage people. They are totally docile people and not capable of hurting a fly – as long as they are only introverts. They do not manipulate people. They have no intention to hurt anyone. In contrast a sociopath is nothing but docile. They can be dangerous but are often simply callous and disregard feelings of others.

Mary Godit was an efficient manager in Oskin & Oskin. She smiled at everyone and wished them on every occasion. Don't you think she would be a likeable person? She wasn't. Everyone in the office hated her. She was known to be a nice person as long as no one crossed her path. She used to lose her temper and get quite angry if anyone questioned her. Mary once fired an employee on the day that woman lost her husband in an accident. "Look, I don't care whether she lost her husband or child", she is known to have remarked. She was obviously a heartless person and going by the general impression no one could live with her, but surprisingly she was a happily married woman with a child who was seven years old. Mary gushed about her family on every occasion. No one knew about her parents. There were rumors that her father was a drunkard who used to beat up the children regularly. Her childhood seemed to be a bit messed up.

Her boss seemed to like her since she was efficient. If only she would stop staring like a vixen, he would comment. She had a scary unwavering stare which was difficult or even impossible to stare down. To compensate for the scary stare she had a beautiful smile. She was charming and articulate. Sometimes she lost her temper but her boss assumed it was stress. After all, who doesn't suffer from stress and anxiety?

Mary was also a compulsive liar. She lied in situations where there was no need for it. Her boss was perplexed whenever he caught her lying. Again, he forgave her because her lies seemed harmless otherwise. Some sociopaths are delusional and believe their own lies.

Mary, on her part never bothered about any of these things. She was fine with any situation as long as it benefitted her. She felt no shame when called out for lying.

She just shrugged all insinuations away. Nothing seemed to stick to her – just flowed way like water from a duck's back.

Mary is a typical sociopath. She manipulated everyone around her. She was simply not affected by what others said about her. She seemed to have no remorse. These are the traits which you must look out for. Sociopath's do not feel normal emotions. They do as they like without caring for the consequences, but they are also sly. They will behave like a kitten when facing superiors. They will stop short of breaking the law. Mary could fire an employee at the worst time possible but still feel righteous. Yes, she got angry and aggressive at times, but who doesn't? But in her case the anger was way beyond what the situation demanded. This is another sign of a sociopath. They get enraged and fly off the handle when confronted. They display uncontrolled rage at some times which to another person may seem unlike their normal smiling personality. If anyone in your group bursts into anger without warning, you can start guessing whether he or she is a sociopath.

The habit of lying is typical of a sociopath. They lie easily and often. They feel no shame if discovered. Don't get carried away by their efficiency. They can be highly productive at work. With their manipulative behavior they rise up the corporate ladder quickly. You will find them as lawyers and financial analysts since these jobs require a personality which can take risks. Sociopaths never panic. They don't possess the nerve required for feeling emotions like panic.

Sociopaths, like Mary, do feel emotions within a group. They may feel emotionally close to someone in the family or the entire family. You will be misled if you think that sociopaths will feel the same about others. They are actually quite the opposite. Sociopaths can be identified by this dichotomy in their behavior. If anyone you know shows this kind of behavior it must raise a red flag.

One of the pointers of a sociopath is their lack of remorse. They will look blankly at an incident which will generally elicit a shocked response from a normal person. This is not a one off incident but repeated continuously by sociopaths. They will do anything to climb up the social and professional ladder. Sometimes they will commit crimes punishable by law if they feel that it will go undetected. They will bend the rules to their advantage. They are extremely manipulative and consider their charm as a weapon to seduce others to do their bidding. They will become violent if things don't turn out to be what they want. This alternative behavior, between seduction and violence is a sure sign of a sociopath.

Some sociopaths suffer from a delusion of greatness. They think no end of themselves. They may even delude themselves to be good in professions for which they have no real talent. Some may suffer from the Christ or Jesus syndrome. They act and behave like messiahs. Such people have a religious background.

Sociopaths like to listen to their own voice. They ignore what other person is saying in a conversation. They look at themselves in the mirror more often than others. This narcissistic behavior is one of the signs of a sociopath.

If a person has no childhood friends it may indicate that he or she is a sociopath. Does a person explain to you in detail why he has no friends from the past? Sociopaths will go to extreme lengths to convince you why they don't have childhood friends.

If you are dating sociopath, he will try to stop you communicating with other friends. They will dissuade you from talking to others and fully focus on them alone. The problem with such behavior is that sociopaths will break a relationship without blinking and you will be left with no friends.

Sociopaths are seldom dangerous and usually never break the law. They learn quite fast and avoid situations which can put them behind bars. However, they are impulsive and can commit a crime like any other person. Unlike psychopaths, they are not serial killers. Though this example is that of a woman, it is men who more often suffer from sociopathy.

It is not necessary that sociopaths have a balanced family life. Sociopaths are seen to have multiple marriages and divorce marred by violent behavior at home. Not surprisingly people suffering from sociopathy pair up with others with similar disorders. You must look at the childhood history of your associates, partners and neighbors, if possible, to understand the genesis of their behavior. Childhood sexual abuse, living in poverty and also a background of verbal and physically abusive parenthood are indicators of likely sociopathy. People like Mary may contribute financially to charity but are seldom a part of such communities. They like to give for charity more because it will make them look better in the eyes of peers than genuine generosity and compassion.

A female sociopath is likely to marry at an early age. They are also prone to selecting mates who are violent and anti-social. Their marriages don't last long but sociopath woman don't seem to learn from their past mistakes and choose a person with similar profile. Abortions and child birth at an early age is indicated in cases of sociopathy.

Chapter 5: How To Spot A Sociopath?

As already mentioned, spotting a sociopath may be like looking for a needle in a hay stack. Not that they are small in number – 4% of the general population can be termed as sociopaths. The problem arises when you may look at everyone suspiciously trying to evaluate their status as a probable sociopath. We are as much different psychologically as we are physically. Each one of us is unique. Some may have some quirky lifestyle which may be mistaken as sociopathic. People can behave differently without begetting the label of a sociopath. So, what sets sociopaths apart from others whom we consider normal? How to spot one?

Sociopaths never learn, in the sense that normal human beings test the limits of law but remain within its boundaries. You may tell small lies, go late for work and take a long time at the water cooler. These are attempts to subvert the law in a small way, but when a person breaks the law by intentionally driving in a drunken state, knowing fully well that they may cause a fatal accident, they cross the boundary. Sociopaths land in trouble because of their scant regard for social taboos and laws.

You should not mistake introvert as a sociopath. An introvert is simply a shy being who does not have the traits to engage people. They are totally docile people and not capable of hurting a fly – as long as they are only introverts. They do not manipulate people. They have no intention to hurt anyone. In contrast a sociopath is nothing but docile. They can be dangerous but are often simply callous and disregard feelings of others.

Mary Godit was an efficient manager in Oskin & Oskin. She smiled at everyone and wished them on every occasion. Don't you think she would be a likeable person? She wasn't. Everyone in the office hated her. She was known to be a nice person as long as no one crossed her path. She used to lose her temper and get quite angry if anyone questioned her. Mary once fired an employee on the day that woman lost her husband in an accident. "Look, I don't care whether she lost her husband or child", she is known to have remarked. She was obviously a heartless person and going by the general impression no one could live with her, but surprisingly she was a happily married woman with a child who was seven years old. Mary gushed about her family on every occasion. No one knew about her parents. There were rumors that her father was a drunkard who used to beat up the children regularly. Her childhood seemed to be a bit messed up.

Her boss seemed to like her since she was efficient. If only she would stop staring like a vixen, he would comment. She had a scary unwavering stare which was difficult or even impossible to stare down. To compensate for the scary stare she had a beautiful smile. She was charming and articulate. Sometimes she lost her temper but her boss assumed it was stress. After all, who doesn't suffer from stress and anxiety?

Mary was also a compulsive liar. She lied in situations where there was no need for it. Her boss was perplexed whenever he caught her lying. Again, he forgave her because her lies seemed harmless otherwise. Some sociopaths are delusional and believe their own lies.

Mary, on her part never bothered about any of these things. She was fine with any situation as long as it benefitted her. She felt no shame when called out for lying.

She just shrugged all insinuations away. Nothing seemed to stick to her – just flowed way like water from a duck's back.

Mary is a typical sociopath. She manipulated everyone around her. She was simply not affected by what others said about her. She seemed to have no remorse. These are the traits which you must look out for. Sociopath's do not feel normal emotions. They do as they like without caring for the consequences, but they are also sly. They will behave like a kitten when facing superiors. They will stop short of breaking the law. Mary could fire an employee at the worst time possible but still feel righteous. Yes, she got angry and aggressive at times, but who doesn't? But in her case the anger was way beyond what the situation demanded. This is another sign of a sociopath. They get enraged and fly off the handle when confronted. They display uncontrolled rage at some times which to another person may seem unlike their normal smiling personality. If anyone in your group bursts into anger without warning, you can start guessing whether he or she is a sociopath.

The habit of lying is typical of a sociopath. They lie easily and often. They feel no shame if discovered. Don't get carried away by their efficiency. They can be highly productive at work. With their manipulative behavior they rise up the corporate ladder quickly. You will find them as lawyers and financial analysts since these jobs require a personality which can take risks. Sociopaths never panic. They don't possess the nerve required for feeling emotions like panic.

Sociopaths, like Mary, do feel emotions within a group. They may feel emotionally close to someone in the family or the entire family. You will be misled if you think that sociopaths will feel the same about others. They are actually quite the opposite. Sociopaths can be identified by this dichotomy in their behavior. If anyone you know shows this kind of behavior it must raise a red flag.

One of the pointers of a sociopath is their lack of remorse. They will look blankly at an incident which will generally elicit a shocked response from a normal person. This is not a one off incident but repeated continuously by sociopaths. They will do anything to climb up the social and professional ladder. Sometimes they will commit crimes punishable by law if they feel that it will go undetected. They will bend the rules to their advantage. They are extremely manipulative and consider their charm as a weapon to seduce others to do their bidding. They will become violent if things don't turn out to be what they want. This alternative behavior, between seduction and violence is a sure sign of a sociopath.

Some sociopaths suffer from a delusion of greatness. They think no end of themselves. They may even delude themselves to be good in professions for which they have no real talent. Some may suffer from the Christ or Jesus syndrome. They act and behave like messiahs. Such people have a religious background.

Sociopaths like to listen to their own voice. They ignore what other person is saying in a conversation. They look at themselves in the mirror more often than others. This narcissistic behavior is one of the signs of a sociopath.

If a person has no childhood friends it may indicate that he or she is a sociopath. Does a person explain to you in detail why he has no friends from the past? Sociopaths will go to extreme lengths to convince you why they don't have childhood friends.

If you are dating sociopath, he will try to stop you communicating with other friends. They will dissuade you from talking to others and fully focus on them alone. The problem with such behavior is that sociopaths will break a relationship without blinking and you will be left with no friends.

Sociopaths are seldom dangerous and usually never break the law. They learn quite fast and avoid situations which can put them behind bars. However, they are impulsive and can commit a crime like any other person. Unlike psychopaths, they are not serial killers. Though this example is that of a woman, it is men who more often suffer from sociopathy.

It is not necessary that sociopaths have a balanced family life. Sociopaths are seen to have multiple marriages and divorce marred by violent behavior at home. Not surprisingly people suffering from sociopathy pair up with others with similar disorders. You must look at the childhood history of your associates, partners and neighbors, if possible, to understand the genesis of their behavior. Childhood sexual abuse, living in poverty and also a background of verbal and physically abusive parenthood are indicators of likely sociopathy. People like Mary may contribute financially to charity but are seldom a part of such communities. They like to give for charity more because it will make them look better in the eyes of peers than genuine generosity and compassion.

A female sociopath is likely to marry at an early age. They are also prone to selecting mates who are violent and anti-social. Their marriages don't last long but sociopath woman don't seem to learn from their past mistakes and choose a person with similar profile. Abortions and child birth at an early age is indicated in cases of sociopathy.

Chapter 6: Psychopathy

What is a psychopath? Is it possible to believe that a person with psychopathic tendencies is actually born this way without being able to prevent their behavior? The psychology community believes psychopaths are born. Many studies including those by PhD Kent Kiehl indicate there are areas of the brain that are underdeveloped or incorrectly developed that lead to psychopathic behavior. Kiehl is one of the expert psychologists that have been using MRIs and CAT scans to support diagnoses of psychopathy. Many, not all, but several of the diagnosed psychopaths have shown the emotional and impulse regions of the brain are underdeveloped when compared to a "normal" individual.

Psychopaths are still going to have the same personality traits as defined in the DSM V for antisocial personality disorder. A psychopath will be unable to form proper emotional attachments with anyone, although they do have the ability to fake their emotions in the right situations. Most often their emotional attachments are artificial with shallow relationships that allow the person to manipulate the person in a way that would benefit the psychopath. Although not a psychological definition, a psychopath is someone who can see people as chess pieces that can be used or discarded as it befits the psychopath's goals. They are able to behave in this manner because most do not feel guilt—no matter how much they hurt others.

A number of psychopaths have been able to hold normal jobs for a long period of time. They even seem to have loving relationships with their significant others and care greatly for their children if they have any. Despite this, the emotions are artificial. It is more about appearance to look trustworthy and capable than the emotional relationship. Psychologists studying psychopaths often find a charming person that is well educated and capable of learning on their own. As Pinel recorded in the 1700s, individuals with psychopathic traits are of high intelligence, without a show of insanity or delirium. They are capable of knowledge in terms of right or wrong; however it is the impulses and lack of empathy that can lead the person to doing something against societal rules.

Not all psychopaths will become criminals or exhibit criminal behavior. If someone does decide to act in a criminal way it is with minimal risk to themselves. Often the crime is planned out carefully, with several contingencies to ensure that they are not caught. Being caught or not caught for the crime does not mean police do not suspect the person of the crime they committed. It is simply a lack of concrete evidence that would convict the criminal in a court of law. Any reasonable doubt can ensure the person is not convicted of the crime no matter how guilty they may be.

Genetic Studies and Psychopathy Facts

According to PhD Kent Kiehl, one in four of the maximum security inmates is a psychopath. Studies also indicate about 30 million people in the world today are psychopaths when assessed by the DSM V criteria. Thankfully according to experts like Kiehl 77% of USA psychopaths are currently in jail. Another startling fact that Kiehl revealed is a psychopath is born about every 47 seconds.

Kiehl provided his research in his own book called The Psychopath Whisperer. He is well known in psychology circles due to his extensive studies of humans displaying psychopathic behavior. He supports the theory that psychopaths are born rather than being made by their environment. He revealed that numerous parents write to him about their children displaying antisocial behaviors in which there is no remorse or change in behavior even after different levels of discipline.

Of course Kiehl is not the only PhD psychologist who has studied the behavior of psychopaths and come to the same conclusion. In the 1980s Professor Adrian Raine, a British neuroscientist started a study scanning murderers brains. Looking at the pre-frontal cortex of the brain which is known for controlling emotional impulses Raine and his team discovered a reduction in activity. When the brain was showed pictures of horrific events and situations that would normally bring about guilt, empathy and strong emotions the pre-frontal cortex was not as active. However, the amygdala was over active.

This is the area of the brain scientists have linked to emotions such as rage and anger. It is also the area known for providing impulse control.

At the time and with the murderer Donta Page as part of their study, Raine began to think the trouble may be linked with physical abuse. The pre-frontal cortex in a baby is more prone to injury. Shaking a baby could damage this part of the brain leaving the individual unable to properly form attachments or control impulses. Donta Page was also abused throughout childhood. Yet, blaming abuse on all cases where individuals turned out as murderers did not work because not everyone abused became a murderer and some not abused did murder people.

After nearly 15 years of research a discovery was made that would prove psychopathy is a born trait. A family from the Netherlands was studied because the men had a long history of violence. In 1993 it was discovered, with the help of genetic research that all the men lacked a specific gene. It is a gene known to produce MAOA, an enzyme that regulates neurotransmitters known to help with impulse control. The lack of the MAOA gene has been linked with a predisposition towards violence.

Although individuals may lack this gene or have others that are linked with psychopathic behavior there is still a necessity for environmental factors to influence a person one way or the other. Jim Fallon is one example. He is a respected professor with a long list of murderers on his family tree. He decided to undergo genetic testing, finding several genes that are linked with psychopathic tendencies. Yet, he is not a murderer. He firmly believes his genes did not affect his behavior because of a happy, safe, and loving childhood.

Research is only 35 years in the making in terms of psychopaths and genetics. No conclusion can be drawn as to whether it is more of the environment a child grows up in or genes they inherit from their parents that will turn them into a violent psychopath. What is known is a person diagnosed with a psychopathic disorder is more likely to commit a new crime when they are released from prison and those who are not caught will continue to commit the same crimes.

Chapter 7: Diagnosing A Personality Disorder

Due to the high level of confusion between mental illnesses and personality disorders it can be extremely difficult to diagnose a condition without medical assistance. In addition, there are so many different personality disorders it can be relatively easy to misdiagnose someone as their symptoms are similar to a different disorder. The following guide will provide you with information regarding how to know if your loved one potentially has a disorder and to narrow it to a specific one. This will enable you to attempt to obtain a professional diagnosis. If you are not convinced that the medical professional has isolated the right disorder then you should seek a second opinion. It is essential to know what you are dealing with to ensure you are best prepared for looking after your loved one and that they have the best chance of a fulfilling life.

Symptoms

The most important thing to remember regarding the symptoms of a personality disorder is that the symptoms must have been visible for an extended period of time. There are times in everyone's life when you may feel overwhelmed, stressed and anxious. You may respond badly to people, become aggressive and even avoid social situations. This does not mean you have a personality disorder; instead it means that you are human and going through a difficult time. Only when these symptoms have been present for at least six months, and preferably a year, will you have a problem that needs help dealing with.

The most common symptoms which will be visible regardless of which disorder you have are:

- Intense Emotions

Anyone suffering with a mood disorder is likely to have very quick mood swings. Their mood will often be at an extreme, either incredibly happy, or incredibly angry, or even suicidal and depressed. A mood can last for seconds, minutes or even days. What defines these intense emotions is the speed at which the mood can change; it is akin to flicking a switch; this is combined with the extremity of the reaction. This is usually far worse than the situation demands.

- Behaviour

The second symptom involves the behavioural patterns of someone with a personality disorder. Their behaviour is likely to be very impulsive and can often be seen as harmful to either them or others, this is categorized by the fact that they do not seem, to acknowledge or even be aware of the danger and its consequences.

There are some personality disorders which are categorized by the opposite. People who appear to have a complete inability to do anything outside of the norm; these people are likely to have compulsive behaviour. They will probably have a set routine and will stick to it regardless of what else is going on; they can become very anxious and upset if they are not able to complete their routines.

• Relationships

In general people with personality disorders have difficulty in forming, building and maintaining a relationship. Much of this is connected with their fear of insufficient self-worth and their distrust, or paranoia, towards others. Generally a close bond is retained with family members as they have grown up with them before the condition became an issue. However, these relationships can be based on a fragile trust and can easily be damaged.

- Self-worth

One if the common denominator's across the entire range of personality disorders is the lack of self-worth. Many personality disorders emphasise a feeling of low self-esteem, an inability to achieve things that 'normal' people can and a frustration with their own perception of life and how they are unable to improve their prospects. Many of these factors are resolvable but, if you are suffering from a personality disorder you may not be able to see how this is possible and instead dwell on the negatives.

- Abandonment Issues

Those with personality disorders tend to have fragile egos and will spend much of their time convinced that they will be abandoned. This will be the case even if there has been no sign or evidence of this being an option. This issue can become a huge problem if left untreated as it is likely that they will not be able to leave your side for more than a few moments at a time. Even suggesting that you might want five minutes peace can be taken the wrong way!

• Aggression

Unfortunately, many people with personality disorders become frustrated at the inability to do simple tasks or achieve their own goals. This can translate into anger and they are likely to lash out at those closest to them. This is because they feel safest around them and are most likely to be themselves. This aggression will, most likely, disappear as fast as it arrives, but, it can cause significant damage and may leave you feeling unsafe alone with them.

- Friendships

Another classic sign that someone has a personality disorder is the making and breaking of friendships. Each friendship will be made quickly and will be broken just as quickly. This is often seen in children's relationships with each other and is often not a cause for concern. However, if this continues into their adult years it is symbolic of a personality disorder.

- Responsibility

Perhaps one of the biggest clues is an inability to accept responsibility for their actions. People with personality disorders tend to have less empathy and awareness of people and the world around them. They often do not see how their actions can affect others; as such, they are oblivious to the responsibility of their actions and are often surprised if asked to justify or explain a course of action. To someone with a personality disorder there are often very few choices, a black and white world makes it easy to decide a path; regardless of the potential consequences.

Living with a personality disorder is not easy for the sufferer or the family and loved ones who are trying to help them. However, there is a vast amount of help and advice available; there are even whole online communities dedicated to making your life better and more manageable; whether you are the carer or the sufferer.

As mentioned, there are symptoms which are specific to certain disorders, but if your loved one, or even yourself, have displayed the above characteristics for an extended period of time you should seek professional help.

It has become increasingly common for medical professionals to talk about the best course of action without actually diagnosing you with a personality disorder. As there are many similarities between the various personality disorders there is a risk of the wrong diagnosis being given. Alongside this there remains a stigma attached to the idea that you have a personality disorder; labelling the condition does nothing to help deal with the issues but it can be seen as insulting by the sufferer. It can also undermine their condition and lose the trust or respect of the sufferer in their doctor. This is particularly true when dealing with people suffering from a disorder in the category C range who are already anxious.

Instead, the focus of your doctor will be to refer you to a specialist whom, they believe, can help you explore the issue further. This is most likely to start with counselling to both help them understand your issues and to build a trusting relationship which will assist in the longer term treatment.

Of course, there are those who prefer to have a name for their illness as this helps them to define their issues and tackle them. It can be a difficult call for a doctor to make!

Diagnosing a personality disorder must be started by either the sufferer or a loved one. Once you realise that your loved one has been displaying the symptoms for some time you will need to establish which symptoms are predominate and for how long they have been a part of their life. You will then be able to consult this book, the internet and even online forums to assist you in making your own diagnosis of the issue.

The next step will be to visit your doctor to start the process of having your diagnosis confirmed. As mentioned, your doctor may refer you without confirming a diagnosis. If having a name for the disorder is important to you then you should press your doctor for a preliminary diagnosis.

Once you have seen the specialist you will be in a position to start treatment, whilst there is no magic pill which will cure a personality disorder there are medications which can help. Prescription drugs can be used to help control mood swings and to decrease the amount of stress and anxiety you place your body under. Alongside this it is highly likely that there will be counselling sessions. These will be aimed at helping you too understand where your disorder stems from, how to recognise the signs that you are about to have a mood swing, or become aggressive and what methods you can utilise to control or prevent it. It is impossible to provide a time frame regarding how long it may take for you to gain complete control of your life and learn to live with your disorder; every case is different. The most important part is to acknowledge that you have an issue and take your first steps towards getting better by visiting the doctor; it is this which can be the hardest step of all.

Chapter 8: Shades Of A Psychopath

"In situations of captivity the perpetrator becomes the most powerful person in the life of the victim, and the psychology of the victim is shaped by the actions and beliefs of the perpetrator."

— Judith Lewis Herman, Trauma and Recovery: The Aftermath of Violence - From Domestic Abuse to Political Terror

Do Psychopaths Know Love?

You are probably curious about whether or not psychopaths can feel love and other emotions. This largely depends on the individual and the severity of their mental disorder. While psychopaths can't feel love and have relationships for the sake of happiness, they do it for different reasons.

Why psychopaths want relationships

In general, psychopaths lack emotion or experience it only to a slight degree. Still, some psychopaths do show a normal degree or even hypersensitivity to some feelings. It makes the answer to the question of whether or not psychopaths can love complicated.

They need attachment

The first thing to address is the shallow nature of psychopath's emotion. Psychopaths have a different degree of sensitivity to different feelings. They are shallow when it comes to guilt, fear, and empathy. Still, they can experience happiness, but only a minimal amount. This is not the same intensity of the emotion as the ordinary person's. However, sensations like rage and anger are something that psychopaths can feel intensely.

Whether or not psychopaths love and how much are they capable of love depends on the degree of psychopathy. A psychopath's ability to love depends on the level of psychopathy and some degree of attachment is possible. Still, they are not likely to create secure connections. However, they will want to receive and take love, although they are unable to give it back. Despite this, psychopaths have relationships and marriages as a way of keeping up appearances.

They need company

Most psychopaths are aware that there is something that makes them different from the rest of the world and that they are emotionally detached. This causes them a lot of suffering and dissatisfaction. However, this suffering results from a desire to have attention, which replaces a healthy human desire for connection. This happens because of abuse or neglect.

They need comfort

Psychopaths experience grief like other people. In fact, the death of someone they consider to be close to them can induce the same amount of pain and sadness as to the ordinary person. Some might cry and have similar emotional responses to trauma as other people. However, to them, trauma is often suppressed.

Psychopaths can also be hypersensitive to specific emotions. This often goes for their sense of control, loneliness, hopelessness, and powerlessness. Psychopaths feel a certain sense of happiness when they are committing acts that go against the social norm. They are easily bored, so they strive for stimulation.

How Psychopaths Use 'Love' to Manipulate?

Psychopaths manipulate with love, which makes their impact on their family's well-being that much more severe. With no emotional capacity, many psychopaths are skillful in making people do what they want for the sake of love. Most people associate psychopathy with criminals and murderers. However, not all psychopaths are prone to criminal behavior. While antisocial behavior, arrogance, dishonesty, and the disregard for others are common traits of a psychopath, their exterior is often a stark contrast to their personality.

Emotional Machiavellians

Psychopaths manipulate using their emotional intelligence. Emotional intelligence embodies a person's ability to manage, understand, and identify emotions in themselves and others. In general, we think of people who are more emotionally intelligent as kind and good to others. The truth is, emotional intelligence also has a dark side in the person's ability to manipulate emotions.

A dark side to emotional intelligence manifests in a psychopath's ability to use the knowledge of others' emotions to manipulate. Psychopaths can talk around their manipulation even when they are called out on it. They will find a way to alter or at least try to find a way to change the person's perception of the situation. In general, they use emotional intelligence for their own gain.

Research confirms that psychopaths can portray perfect empathy without significant inner response. They seem as empathetic as any other person. However, this response is only superficial. When analyzing the brains of psychopaths, researchers tried to see whether their minds will be activated by the sights of physical and emotional hurt. The results of this research suggest that psychopaths had a lower response in their brains to the suffering of others. This explains why they can commit crimes or harm other people without feeling guilty. Simultaneously, they can look charming. Regardless of circumstances, they can put on a smile and appear engaging if they feel like they have something to gain. The ability of emotional disguise enables psychopaths to fake love when they have zero actual feeling.

Psychopaths mainly use deception for manipulation. To manipulate with love, psychopaths use the following strategies:

Charm

Charm is one of the main character traits of psychopaths. They know how to act to gain an advantage. They operate in a smooth manner. Because of their low emotional responses, they often trick the lie detectors. They stay calm when pressured. In that state, they tell the most incredible stories that are straight-up lies.

Another way to catch the psychopath who is using their term against you is to notice if they deflect conversations. They will try to switch your focus from the topic of conversation to flattery. They will use affection to divert the conversation. With a loving face and a gentle touch, they will sway you from questioning their stories and their motives.

Flawed logic

Psychopaths often manipulate using false analogies. They use figurative ways of speech to persuade you into inaccurate, irrational ideas.

● For example, if a psychopath discovers your desire for a family and the insecurity in your ability to have one, they'll tell you that love can overcome any obstacles. This way, they'll sway you into forgetting about your insecurities and starting a family with them. Once your insecurities start getting the best of you, they'll use them in their favor. If you believe you're an incompetent parent, they'll lead you to think you shouldn't do anything without their approval. That includes handling money, child-rearing, and getting back to work. Opposite to that, a genuine person would acknowledge your insecurities and wait until you work through them to start a family. The first person wants you weak, and the other wants you strong.

Manipulators can spark a strong emotional response in you. For example, if a psychopath wants to get you to lend them money, they will use metaphors related to love that depict that the love is worth all the risk. You'll do something for them that goes against your beliefs, like getting a loan you can't pay off. They will use false analogies that make immoral and unwise actions justified.

Insult and slander

When pushed into a corner, psychopaths will use insults and slander. They will slander one's reputation to get out of a bad situation. Psychopaths also use slander to discredit opponents, including your family.

Emotional fog

A psychopath will find a way to make you feel guilty for their wrongdoings. When you're about to uncover a psychopath's lies, they will use every tool they have to sway you from doing so. For this, they will use circumlocution. They will beat around the bush, avoiding answering directly to a straightforward question. Usually, they'll try to change the subject or simply lie. If they notice that the lie isn't being effective, they will try to change the subject.

In a confrontation, they will resort to either criticism or flattery. This is all done to cloud your judgment.

Evasiveness

Psychopaths manipulate with evasiveness. They will answer vaguely to a direct question. This way, they avoid answering specific questions about themselves and their actions.

Deflecting guilt

Psychopath's first response to being called out for something that they've done will be to blame someone else. They will blame another person even if it entails lying. If not you, they will blame their family, friends, society, or the entirety of humanity. No matter what evidence you present them with, they won't act accountable.

Still, keep in mind that being manipulative doesn't make one a psychopath. Manipulation is a tool many people use to achieve what they want. The best way to describe how psychopaths manipulate with love is to say that they use your emotional vulnerability and attachment to them to deflect from real facts.

Lies

This leads us to the next behavior typical for psychopaths, which is lying. Lying is another one of the main traits of a psychopath. When beating around the bush or manipulating doesn't do the trick, that they will fabricate details. You can catch these lies because they tend to change their stories a lot. They will also fabricate the information so that your mind is now deflected from the question you asked. This is a method of improvisation to deflect your attention from them and their actions to something else using your emotions.

Being emotionally manipulated is perhaps the most toxic and harmful effect of being in a relationship with a psychopath. They will use your love for them to make you believe them over anyone else. They will do this by isolating you from other people in your life. This is also a strategy to deflect from revealing actual facts they are being asked about or accepting responsibility for their actions. When they have you wrapped around their finger in a codependent relationship, you will want to believe them over anyone else. If that doesn't work, the psychopath will also prey on your feelings of hopelessness and emotional attachment. If confronted with facts, they will play upon the fact that you will be unhappy without them, using emotional blackmail to get you to regret questioning them.

Emotional deception

Emotional deception is another way in which psychopaths use emotions to manipulate. They use one person to lie to another person. They do this by encouraging antagonism. If you hear stories about them from your friend or a family member, and you confront a psychopath with this information, they will use everything they know about your relationship with that other person to stay in control. For example, if your mother informs you that your partner is cheating on you, they will deflect the story from cheating to highlighting the problems you have in the relationship with your mother. They will tell you not to trust her because she's being judgmental and controlling. He will make you think that your parent is trying to get in the way of your happiness. They can make it look like other people are speaking against them because they want to hurt you.

Distorting the truth

Manipulation using the truth is one of the finest forms of manipulation. That is a tactic high-functioning psychopaths often use most often. They will use accurate information for immoral purposes. For example, they can speak about an event that actually happened, but their ulterior goal might be to distance you from your relationships or smear other's reputation in your mind. A psychopath might use something they know from the past of your parents or coworkers, and present it to you in a way for you to question the relationship. In this situation, you can't really accuse them of lying because factually, they are not, but you can accuse them of how they're trying to use the truth.

What to Expect from a Relationship with a Psychopath?

Namely, psychopaths use relationships to benefit themselves in either gratification or money. A psychopath isn't in a relationship with you; it's not so that you can have a happy life together, but instead, it is to dominate and run your life, be in control of your money, and get gain sexual gratification. Whatever their motive is, there is no love in it and it revolves solely around their gain.

All psychopaths use similar strategies in intimate relationships. It's hard to get out of their web because they're good at tearing down your self-esteem and making you believe you're hopeless without them. Sadly, it's hard to notice these traits at first, because Western culture approves of many characteristics that can be described as psychopathic. For example, an egocentric, self-fulfilling way of thinking, ambition without regard to others, and lowering the importance of emotion in business and relationships are only some of the reasons why you may have failed to notice that there is something wrong with your partner.

Stages of psychopathic seduction

If you're in a relationship with a psychopath, you can expect them to act caring at first and then become cold and distant. If you maintain eye contact for a longer time, you will notice that there is no real emotion behind their eyes. In relationships, psychopaths often express predatory behavior. They're also territorial, don't like their belongings touched, and want to dominate. They will act as if certain parts of your home are solely theirs, and you cannot access them. Here are the following stages typical for intimate relationships with psychopaths:

- Seduction
- Love bombing
- Bonding, when they use all the strategies to make you believe like they are your best option
- Trauma bonding

After the last stage, they entrap and eventually discard you.

Seduction

The first stage is the stage of seduction. In this stage, psychopaths read your personality and figure out what kind of partner you want them to be. Next, they shape themselves after that image. They'll transform into any type of personality, depending on whether you prefer a masculine or a more submissive partner, a mature partner or a more child-like partner. In this stage, they will also mimic your behavior so that you feel like they are similar to you. They will copy your body language and even your lifestyle. This way, they gain your trust. They will also mimic the way you dress, the way you speak, the way you smile, your body language, your thoughts and attitudes, and everything else.

They might act according to your aspirations and values. With this, they will use their charm, good manners, and confidence to lure you in. There's a natural attractiveness to confident people, and psychopaths are aware of it. Perhaps they will try to fascinate you with their courageousness, which is actually a display of their careless nature, as discussed earlier.

Love bombing

In this stage, they will try to impress you so that you focus solely on them. They will aim to become your personal hero. They will act in ways to make you idolize them and make the relationship the main focus of your life. They will always go the extra mile with gifts and become your Prince Charming. They will profess love and act protective and caring. It might happen that a person flirting with you professes love slightly too soon when they haven't known you enough. The next time someone confesses their love for you, you can question they know you enough to start feeling like that. In this stage, they will want to make you addicted to their attention. They will aim to make you feel like you need them desperately.

Bonding

In the following state, a psychopath will use bonding based on lies to make you feel like you have now intimately bonded. They will tell you stories of their childhood trauma and make up many dramatic stories that they allegedly haven't told anyone else. These will be false secrets. If you ever tried to track or validate the information that they gave you, you discover that they are untrue. If you ask them directly, they will use all the tactics of deflection mentioned earlier. To fabricate a story, they will use your 'weaknesses.' For example, if you are particularly sensitive to child abuse, they might tell you that they were abused as a child. If you are sensitive to poverty, they will tell you that they used to be poor. If one of your loved ones is sick and that's bothering you, they will tell you that they survived the problematic illness and make you feel like you share a strong bond.

Another important aspect of this is that you will also be telling them your secrets. You will reveal most intimate fears, desires, and experiences, many of which you don't want anyone else to know. A psychopath will listen carefully and wait for the right time to start manipulating you with these experiences and use them against you.

Bonding is the stage in which the psychopath will start to have sex with you. With an emotional background, sex will only further deepen the bond. Psychopaths are often intense in intimacy, which can be either gratifying or start to get violent. In sex, they will either act on your desires or try to establish their own dominance, depending on your personal traits and the type of a psychopath.

However, your intimate relationship is tailored around the goal of making you addicted to him. In this stage, you will be spending a lot of time together and they will fully integrate into your life. You will become addicted to spending time with him and having sex with him. You will start to feel like nothing else matters aside from your relationship.

Trauma bonding

The fourth stage of the relationship with a psychopath is the trauma bond. In this stage, they will slowly start to act like their abusive selves. They may become indifferent, verbally abusive, or even violent. They'll use many strategies to make you emotionally upset. This trauma will only enforce your connection with the abuse and enforce the mind control. The more the psychopath traumatizes you, the more you'll feel hopeless, weak, and dependent on him.

After the love bombing, you will find it hard to believe that he is truly the person he is now showing himself to be. You will want to make up excuses, which will be that you are the one who caused the abuse. The intensity of the bond makes you believe that they are the love of your life and that you can't live without them. In this stage, the abuser starts tearing down your self-esteem and becomes even more dependent. You'll become their slave.

Psychopaths use trauma bonding to absorb intense feelings, which they enjoy. This puts the victim into a state of altered consciousness. You are almost spellbound and in a state of cognitive dissonance. Deep down, you can't believe that someone who used to be so loving is now acting violently. The only way for you to explain it to yourself is to think that something is wrong with you. This is the beginning of your enslavement. From this point on, the psychopath will become more and more abusive, and your self-esteem will be even lower. With your self-esteem diminished, you feel even more emotionally attached to that person.

They will use emotional manipulation to seduce you back into their web whenever they start to feel like they're losing control over you. They will do things to confuse you and make you feel like you're insane. If you used to be a happy, confident person, you can easily start to question your judgment and self-worth.

Entrapment

The next stage is the stage of entrapment in which the psychopath will try to completely isolate you and submit you to their dominance. They will try to establish complete control over your life. They will initiate marriage or get you pregnant so that it's more difficult for you to get a divorce. They will isolate you from other relationships using many manipulative and violent tactics. They will do their best to distance you from your friends, family, and even make you quit your job. Ultimately, when you are all used up and a psychopath has nothing else to gain from you, they will leave you. This can happen either because of sickness, age or poverty. They will abandon you once you become irreparably damaged by the abuse, and you're of no use to them.

The Dangers of Relationships with Psychopaths, Sociopaths, and Narcissists

Being in a relationship with a mentally unstable person can have devastating effects. Under the influence of psychopathic manipulation, your health can deteriorate, your work and relationships might suffer, and your life can be overall ruined. Here are the biggest dangers from being in a relationship with a psychopath:

- **Emotional and psychological abuse.** Psychopaths use numerous techniques to cloud their victims' judgment and ruin their self-esteem, such as:

  o Verbal and emotional manipulation

  o Insults

  o Passive-aggressiveness

  o Staging situations and conversations for the victim to question their reason and sanity

  o Avoiding to give answers to straightforward questions

These behaviors lead to mental confusion in a victim. Because the abuser acts in unpredictable and ambiguous ways, you are always tense and on edge, not knowing when you'll say or do something to upset the abuser. This can have severe effects on your health and even cause anxiety and depression.

• **Physical and sexual abuse.**
Psychopaths are prone to physical and
sexual abuse and violence. They will use
violence to establish control and
dominance over the victim. They are very
skillful in disguising the abuse using
manipulation so that the victim is often
unaware of being abused. When
confronted about their behavior, a
psychopath will blame the victim for his
actions.

• **Damage to your career and finances.**
Psychopaths enjoy taking away the
financial freedom from their victims.
They'll either sabotage their partner's
career, or abuse their funds. It's common
for psychopaths to cause a great deal of
financial damage, including overspending,
getting their victims to take out a loan only
to squander the money on their own fun
and luxuries, and even taking the money
for false investments.

- **Isolation**. Psychopaths tend to isolate their victims and get in the way of their friendly and familial relationships. In particular, a psychopath will sabotage any relationship of their victim's that goes against their interest.

The Worst-Case Scenario

Violent psychopaths can have a severe and life-threatening impact on their victims. Some of the most dangerous outcomes of a relationship with a psychopath include:

- **Injury and death.** Violent psychopaths are no strangers to putting their partner's life at risk. Depending on the degree of psychopathy, a victim can be attacked and killed in an outburst of rage, or as a reaction to abandoning the abuser. On the other hand, psychopaths also use systematic poisoning and other strategies to put their victim's life in danger. This will happen when a psychopath has used their victim to the point of losing interest.

- **Health problems.** Living in constant fear, trauma, and stress can diminish the health of the victim. Anxiety, panic attacks, cardiovascular diseases, and other health problems that result from chronic stress, are only some of the health problems a victim of abuse can face.

- **Depression and suicide.** Living with constant abuse can cause victims to fall into depression or even commit suicide. The nature of the psychopathic abuse is such to destroy the self-esteem of a victim and make them feel like leaving the abuser is not an option.

How to Protect Yourself?

To protect yourself from psychopathic abuse, it's important to stay focused on your own health and safety. Here's what you should do if you suspect being exposed to psychopathic abuse:

Be safe

Do everything you can to distance yourself from the abuser. Open up about your situation to friends and family, and ask for police protection. If you fear for your safety, report the abuser to the authorities and request a restraining order.

Avoid them at all costs

The chances are that a psychopathic abuser won't let go of you easily. You may fall into temptation to meet them and talk to them, but this could be dangerous. If you doubt you'll resist talking to the abuser, make sure you're never alone and that you have someone by your side to talk you out of it.

Prioritize yourself

The best way to protect yourself is to make yourself your own priority. Avoid making your relationships a priority in your life. Instead, to recover from the abuse, focus on healing. Make your doctor's appointments, therapy sessions, treatment, and recovery, the primary focus.

Be spiritual

Understand the person's character traits and don't try to change them. Giving up on trying to change a person has a deeper impact than you might think. The roots of your vulnerability lie in the refusal to believe that some people just can't change. This way of thinking has a lot to do with your state of mind, which will be further discussed throughout this book.

Chapter 9: Spotting Manipulators In Relationships

Knowing your enemy is always the first rule in any plan to defeat or control. As previously mentioned, mind manipulators work in under handed and deceptive ways. They are always not what they seem. They often wait to become well-established in a relationship before showing their true colors. It may take a long while for manipulated people to realize the pernicious cycle they are going through. When they finally did, their dreams, confidence, relationships and sense of self are already shattered, and everything is a little too late to recover. Like in the case of serious disease wherein early diagnosis is crucial, determining if you're in a manipulative relationship or situation is the first crucial step to get free from its shackles. In this chapter, the practical ways to find out if you're being manipulated, as well as the common traits of manipulators and their reasons for manipulation, shall be discussed.

Who Are the Manipulators?

There are two (2) kinds of manipulators in our midst. The first type is the conscious manipulator, whose intentions are clearly presented in his/her actions. Conscious manipulators are highly skilled in using force, abuse, wits and charm, blending them together to bend other people's mind and will, often without remorse, in ways that will suit to their liking or purpose. These manipulators are commonly connoisseurs when it comes to pinpointing targets, and can get deeply into someone's emotional state or psyche anytime they wish. They are not necessarily psychologists, but they do know how the mind and emotions of their prey works, and how to successfully twist them (without revealing their true intentions) to serve their purpose.

The second type is the unconscious manipulator. They manipulate people with less (or absent) consciousness of the severity of what they are doing. Their manipulative tendencies stem from their repressed negative emotions, such as insecurity and fear. However, they still see the connection between their tactics in manipulating their targets and the compliance that they receive as ends to their means in the long run, fueling their curiosity and experimentative inclinations. In a way, all conscious manipulators start from being unconscious manipulators. Once the effectiveness of manipulation is revealed to them, they continue exploring this method, and advance in it. They also become more ambitious in pushing their goals farther.

Manipulators are expert chameleons. They can easily and perfectly blend their characters against any given situation. The following are common indications that the person you're dealing with is a manipulator:

1. Extravagant use of praises— Manipulators, especially the conscious ones, believes and abuses the power of praises. Naturally, people like hearing good things about themselves. Manipulators use this weakness, with a perfect application of charm, to handle people, control them and get what they want.

2. Abusive use of reciprocity—In Robert Cialdini's Science of Persuasion, he said that reciprocity is one of the 6 principal social influences that persuade people. For example, as a form of giving back what you owe, if someone gave you a favor, you are more obliged to say YES when that person asked you a favor. Manipulators abuse this power over people to ask them for favors, even if doing so will negatively affect their feelings and compromise their situations.

3. Complete lack (or absence) of trust on others–Manipulators believe more in the evil and vicious streak of people rather than their innate kindness. For them, there is no honor among thieves. Because they themselves are not trustworthy, they do not believe that anyone can be trusted as well.

4. Slave driver– Machiavelli stated that men need masters to govern themselves. Likewise, manipulators believe that other people can only work hard and seriously if they are coerced, albeit unrighteously, to do so.

5. Concrete belief in the practice of illegalities as means to an end– Manipulators have no remorse or hesitation in bending the rules and choosing illegitimacies every single time, in order to get what they want. In fact, illegal actions are always included in their set of plans to reach their goals.

6. Professional liar– Manipulators are more often than not, effective liars. They know how to play the mind and feelings of their targets by using the right choice of words and persuasion. They are also expert in conversational maneuvers, so that no one will hold them responsible for the undesirable results of their own words and promises.

7. Overly narcissistic–A manipulator's sense of self-importance and entitlement is overinflated. Because they feel and believe that they are great people, who are more unique and special than the rest, manipulators are perfectly alright with insensitively abusing the needs and emotions of others.

8. Highly unstable mood swings–Many manipulators use their unstable moods and uncontrolled impulses when controlling other people, particularly those who fear hostility and conflicts. Their emotions border the extremes. One moment they are easy and agreeable individuals, and the next, they are lambasting, angry and vicious control freaks. These manipulative indications are often seen in couples' relationships. When one partner has a constantly fluctuating moods and impulses, the other becomes confused with such behavioral irregularities. Confusion leads to stress, fear and discomfort, which ultimately lead to the person surrendering to every whim of the controlling partner.

9. Unreasonable submissiveness and dependence–This indication is an exact opposite of narcissistic tendencies of a manipulator, but it arrives at the same disheartening aftermath. There are manipulators who portray excessive dependence and helplessness, especially when making decisions, in order to gain care, approval and support from people, and make them do their bidding. The manipulated also has the possibility of becoming a manipulator himself/herself, because he/she feels that since his/her partner cannot decide on his/her own, it is his/her responsibility to control his/her partner's life and handle his/her decisions.

10. Extreme want of attention—There are manipulators whose "tears are poison". In order to get what they want, they use attention-seeking and overly dramatic strategies, which are superficial. Again, people who are scared of conflicts and unwanted attention from the public are easy targets for these types of manipulators.

11.   Passive-aggressive—Some manipulators do not react or resist directly, but intentionally proceeds to becoming a liability or a burden. Intentionally doing the following practices: dawdling, procrastination and lack of concentration, are manipulative tactics as well.

Why Manipulators Do What They Do?

Our actions are largely dependent on our goals, the things that we want to accomplish. For instance, if you want to be at the top of your class, your daily school chores would more or less consist of listening and participating to class discussions, studying well for exams and becoming active in school events. Motives define the attitudes and behaviors of a person. Attitudes and behaviors define the core character of the person. Motives shape the kind of manipulator a person is.

Knowledge of the most possible motives of manipulation is vital to successfully finding out who are the manipulators in your midst. Likewise, effectively identifying manipulators in relationships is a strong weapon to protect yourself from manipulation or from further demise if you're already caught with this trap. Why do manipulators do what they do? Reasons are as many and unique as people, but they can be summarized in a single word: FULFILLMENT.

1. Fulfillment of personal goals. The ends for every means of manipulation are more often than not defined by the goals that the manipulator wants to attain, even if it means breaking other people to do so.

2. Fulfillment of desire for control. Most manipulators do what they do in order to feel a sense of control of things, even if it involves the control of other people's mind and psyche. This is a defense mechanism in order to cover up their most hidden fears, anxieties and insecurities – which they associate with weakness.

Psychologists found this type of mentality in psychopaths, particularly those who have undergone traumatic events in their lives –the turning points that led to their psychopathic nature. Manipulation is an essential motif to crimes committed by psychopaths, because it gives a full grasp of control and superiority over other beings, a complete absence of weakness. Given any situation, manipulators do not believe in a neural stand. For them, they are always right, and others are wrong.

3. Fulfillment of desire for power. There is no drug more addictive than power. The want of power is inherent to every human being, being the highest form of species and all. "Survival of the fittest" is the best definition of a human being's primal instincts. This desire is kept in check usually by conscience, ethics and laws of society, added sometimes by lack of self-confidence.

The manipulator's desire for power is connected to his/her desire for control. Power is the validation of control that the manipulator has on his/her target. For manipulators, power is something finite, which must be possessed by a sole individual (himself/herself), because sharing it to others would mean a decrease in that power and its advantages.

Like in the case of desire for control, a manipulator's ultimate desire for power is just a façade for underlying inferiority and self-esteem issues. Ironically, a manipulator is someone who has a weak self-esteem, but outwardly appears as a strong, bold and egoistic individual.

4. Fulfillment of desire for adventure/experimentation. Boredom and everyday mundaneness are hated by manipulators. Manipulation for expert manipulators is a game – a mind game where real people are played as chess pieces. It gives them satisfaction, and it's a great way for them to exercise their power and control.

Chapter 10: Instructions To Spot Manipulation

We as a whole need to get our necessities met, however controllers utilize wicked techniques. Control is an approach to clandestinely impact somebody with roundabout, misleading, or damaging strategies. Control may appear to be amiable or even agreeable or complimenting, as though the individual has your most noteworthy worry as a primary concern, however in actuality it's to accomplish a ulterior rationale. Different occasions, it's hidden antagonism, and when oppressive strategies are utilized, the goal is only force. You may not understand that you're by and large unwittingly scared.

In the event that you grew up being controlled, it's harder to perceive what's happening, since it feels recognizable. You may have a premonition of uneasiness or outrage, yet on a superficial level the controller may utilize words that are lovely, charming, sensible, or that play on your blame or compassion, so you supersede your impulses and don't have the foggiest idea what to state. Mutually dependent people experience difficulty being immediate and confident and may utilize control to get their direction. They're likewise simple prey for being controlled by narcissists, marginal characters, sociopaths, and different mutually dependent people, including addicts.

Manipulative Tactics

Most loved weapons of controllers are: blame, whining, contrasting, lying, denying (counting reasons and legitimizations), pretending obliviousness, or honesty (the

"Who me!?" guard), fault, pay off, subverting, mind games, suppositions, "foot-in-the-entryway," inversions, enthusiastic coercion, shiftiness, overlooking, counterfeit concern, compassion, statements of regret, sweet talk, and blessings and favors. Controllers regularly use blame by saying straightforwardly or through suggestion, "After everything I've done or you," or constantly acting poor and a defenseless. They may contrast you contrarily with another person or rally fanciful partners to their motivation, saying that, "Everybody" or "All things being equal thus thinks xyz," or "says xyz about you."

A few controllers deny guarantees, arrangements, or discussions, or start a contention and censure you for something you didn't do to get compassion and force. This methodology can be utilized to break a date, guarantee, or understanding. Guardians regularly control with pay off -

everything from, "Finish your supper to get dessert," to "No computer games until your schoolwork is finished." I was paid off with a guarantee of a vehicle, which I required so as to drive to summer school, depending on the prerequisite that I consent to go to the school that my folks had picked as opposed to the one I'd settled on. I generally lamented accepting kickbacks. At the point when you do, it sabotages your confidence. Controllers regularly voice suppositions about your aims or convictions and afterward respond to them as though they were valid so as to legitimize their sentiments or activities, at the same time denying what you a state in the discussion. They may go about as though something has been settled upon or chosen when it hasn't so as to overlook any information or protest you may have.

The "foot-in-the-entryway" procedure is making a little solicitation that you consent to, which is trailed by the genuine solicitation. It's harder to state no, in light of the fact that you've just said yes. The inversion turns your words around to mean something you didn't expect. At the point when you object, controllers reverse the situation on you so that they're the harmed party. Presently it's about them and their objections, and you're on edge. Counterfeit concern is once in a while used to sabotage your choices and trust as alerts or stress over you.

Passionate Blackmail

Passionate extortion is harsh control that may incorporate the utilization of fury, terrorizing, dangers, disgrace, or blame. Disgracing you is a technique to make self-uncertainty and cause you to feel unreliable. It can even be framed in a commendation: "I'm shocked that you, everything being equal, you'd go as far as that!" An exemplary ploy is to alarm you with dangers, outrage, allegations, or desperate alerts, for example, "At your age, you'll never meet any other person in the event that you leave," or "The grass isn't any greener," or playing the person in question: "I'll kick the bucket without you."

Blackmailers may likewise terrify you with outrage, so you penance your necessities and needs. On the off chance that that doesn't work, they here and there unexpectedly change to a lighter state of mind. You're calmed to the point that you're willing to consent to whatever is inquired. They may raise something you feel regretful or embarrassed about from the past as influence to compromise or disgrace you, for example, "I'll tell the youngsters xyz in the event that you do xyz."

Survivors of blackmailers who have certain character issues, for example, fringe or narcissistic PD, are inclined to encounter a mental FOG, which represents Fear, Obligation, and Guilt, an abbreviation made by Susan Forward. The casualty is caused to feel reluctant to cross the controller, feels committed to follow their solicitation, and feels too regretful not to do as such. Disgrace and blame can be utilized straightforwardly with put-downs or allegations that you're "narrow minded" (the more awful bad habit to numerous mutually dependent people) or that "You just consider yourself," "You couldn't care less about me," or that "You have it so natural."

Codependency

Mutually dependent people are seldom self-assured. They may state whatever they think somebody needs to hear to get along or be cherished, yet afterward they do what they need. This is additionally latent forceful conduct. As opposed to respond to an inquiry that may prompt a showdown, they're sly, change the theme, or utilize fault and disavowal (counting reasons and justifications), to abstain from being off-base. Since they discover it so difficult to state no, they may state truly, trailed by objections about how troublesome obliging the solicitation will be.

When stood up to, due to their profound disgrace, mutually dependent people experience issues tolerating duty, so they reject obligation and fault or rationalize or make void expressions of remorse to keep the harmony.

They use appeal and sweet talk and offer kindnesses, help, and blessings to be acknowledged and adored. Analysis, blame, and self-centeredness are likewise used to control to get what they need: "For what reason do you just consider yourself and never ask or help me with my issues? I helped you." Acting like a casualty is an approach to control with blame.

Addicts regularly deny, falsehood, and control to secure their enslavement. Their accomplices additionally control for instance, by stowing away or weakening a fiend's medications or liquor or through other clandestine conduct. They may likewise lie or advise misleading statements to keep away from encounters or control the junkie's conduct.

Inactive hostility

Inactive forceful conduct can likewise be utilized to control. At the point when you experience difficulty saying no, you may consent to things you would prefer not to, and afterward get your way by overlooking, being late, or doing it apathetically. Regularly, inactive animosity is a method of communicating antagonism. Overlooking "deliberately" is helpfully evades what you would prefer not to do and settles the score with your accomplice - like neglecting to get your companion's garments from the cleaners. Now and again, this is done unwittingly, however it's as yet a method of communicating outrage. More unfriendly is offering deserts to your consuming less calories accomplice.

Step by step instructions to Most Effectively Deal With a Psychopath

step by step instructions to most successfully manage an insane person. The main thing to recall is that not all sociopaths are crazy, there are sure characteristics (a considerable lot of them very hazardous) that will be available inside the maniac. This article will start by examining a portion of the characteristics that different the maniac from the ordinary sociopath and it will likewise talk about certain things to remember when someone may be worried about the possibility that that they are managing such a character. Anyone that feelings of dread they are managing such an individual ought to likewise be extremely mindful so as to do however much research as could reasonably be expected on the point.

A sociopath is an individual that is conceived without feeling. A large number of these individuals are very droning since they do not have the cerebrum's normal capacity to start feeling while at the same time communicating with their general surroundings. Since these individuals are without feeling they may be inadequate with regards to the sort of still, small voice that a large portion of the populace has with regards to managing others. With no still,
 small voice an individual is here and there liable to manage others in a negative manner. A few people may take from others or, in extraordinary cases, dismiss others so much that they are even enticed to hurt them. It is significant not to

generalize all sociopaths as maniacal executioners, since some of them figure out how to work regardless of their failure to deliver feeling.

An insane person is an alternate sort of sociopath all together. A significant thing to recall about these individuals is that they may be tricky and able. Individuals with this condition will regularly place a ton of energy and cautious arranging into the negative things that they do. In the event that a customary sociopath harms someone it is regularly an extra existing apart from everything else kind of response. On the off chance that a sociopath harms someone, it is practically sure to state that a considerable measure of arranging went into it.

Another unnerving thing about this kind of character is that these individuals frequently function admirably with others. The sociopath will frequently be droning and deadpan as recently referenced. The sociopath then again is some of the time very viable at faking the kind of feelings that a great many people feel. This is the place where the entirety of the accounts along the lines of "I can't accept someone or other was an executioner, the person appeared to be so decent" originates from. A sociopath isn't commonly going to make companions well, yet a psycho may be very viable at making companions. One thing that individuals need to recall when they are managing someone that gangs this problem is that they can't regularly be trusted. Individuals with this condition are regularly going to lie, and they will be ready to do it very well too. This is the reason numerous individuals with this specific issue are frequently portrayed as manipulative. They are at times ready to invade society very well generally for the opportunity to control people around them.

It is significant that clinical assistance is acquired when managing a sociopath. Not all that much exhortation can be giving for how to viably deal with these individuals due to how hazardous they are! A few people may decide to move as distant from the individual with the issue as they can. An individual ought to most likely make an effort not to face the individual and irritate them. It is critical to always remember that these individuals can carry on brutally when they are irritated. On the off chance that any peruser ever speculates that someone they know is experiencing this problem or the sociopath issue, they should contact an expert for guidance and not go off of what has been perused from the web alone.

It is trusted that everything perusers can more readily see a portion of the things that different an insane person from a standard sociopath. As recently referenced, individuals that spot such a character should look for the guidance of a prepared proficient. This article was composed just to give the peruser a thought of what they are managing. Continuously recall that it isn't remarkable at all for the insane person to be the energy everyone needs and have an enormous group of friends. This stems from their capacity to counterfeit feeling and plan deliberately.

Chapter 11: The Narcissists: Main Characteristics And The Way They Operate

It is quite common to hear that someone is a narcissist, or even to self proclaim it today. This is because narcissism is often confused with confidence and pride. However, this disorder is more complex. True narcissists are overly confident without merit and are destructive to those around them. Research has shown that most narcissists are men. That is, that 75% of all narcissists are men and the rest are women. These are people with an exaggerated view of themselves. Their ideas of superiority are often unrealistic. It is common, for example, for a highly successful person to proclaim their success. This lack of humility, however, does not make them a narcissist. There are a number of characteristics which all narcissists share. A brief description is provided below.

Exaggeration of self-importance and achievements.

The individuals believe that they, and their work, are extremely important. They may even speak of how they achieve everything on their own. They believe that others in their surroundings are incapable and holding them back. For example, they have a job of medium importance but will claim that the company will fail without them. A narcissist will also over emphasize the importance of their achievements. For those who do not know the narcissist for a longer period of time, these stories may even seem true. There is never any evidence to prove their importance, but the narcissist will never admit to it.

Sense of entitlement.

The narcissist believes that they deserve recognition and admiration to an exaggerated degree. However, they rarely do anything worthy of such praise. Nevertheless, they demand constant admiration. Even if they receive praise, it is rarely up to their expectations. They also have this sense of entitlement when it comes to favors or wishes. If their wishes are not met, they feel wronged. For example, they expect that people around them will do as they say without question. Another example is feeling entitled to a promotion, even though they do not deserve one. If their needs are not met they feel cheated, and accuse the other person of being unfair or selfish.

Superiority complex.

Such person strongly believes they are better than almost everyone. They will interact only with people who are highly intelligent, successful or otherwise exceptional. In time, they may view themselves as better than these individuals as well. The narcissist dismisses opinions of others and is known to interrupt without hesitation. They believe that only their opinion is correct and relevant. They rarely listen to anyone and prefer to be at the center of every discussion. A narcissist also doesn't take criticism well. They will react aggressively and hurt the other person on an emotional level.

Lack of empathy.

This is the most relevant trait of a narcissist. Lack of empathy means that they can't relate to the pain or happiness of others. Although they do understand that they have hurt someone, guilt or shame for their actions eludes them. This is, in part, because of their self-righteousness and also because they do not understand or feel the full spectrum of human emotions. Therapists claim that their narcissistic patients often feel numb. This lack of empathy means that they cannot connect to anyone on a deeper level.

Envy.

A narcissist not only envies others and their lives or belongings, but also needs to be envied. They will always aim to have the best and the greatest assets in order to be envied. Their own envy and jealousy is always connected to their need to compete with others. If their friend, for example, has a new phone, they must instantly have the same or a better one. This, of course, they believe will make others envy them. They also believe that everyone is jealous of them even if that is not the case.

Desire to always be in control.

Narcissist will often try to control their partner's emotions. Since they feel more important than others, their own feelings are the most important in the relationship. It is extremely difficult to be with the person who doesn't have high regard of their romantic partner.

They are deceitfully charming.

Narcissists are very charming by nature, so they will show genuine interest in their partner at first. After they get hooked, narcissist's focus shifts back on themselves and they will try to manipulate the other person into keeping them pleased at all times.

Feelings of insecurity.

In reality, their insecurities fuel their tendencies to be narcissistic. They will put their partner down and make them feel less adequate or intelligent just because they have to feel they are better. Also, they will try to make sure they are always superior in the relationship.

Now, let's take a look at narcissistic relationship and how it progresses. A narcissistic relationship is any relationship with one or two narcissists involved. They pick and choose a potential partner that is beautiful, successful, rich or otherwise popular. As they only love themselves, they view the people in their lives as possessions. As with all possessions, the goal is to be envied and further praised.

Narcissists have a set routine of how they behave in a relationship:

The courtship.

The first step is that they charm and impress the person they are interested in. The next thing they always do is place this person on a pedestal. The narcissist becomes infatuated with that person and gives them an excessive amount of love and attention. They pay close attention to what their love interest wants in order to manipulate them. This allows them to become the perfect man or woman.

The actual relationship.

Once they are sure that their partner is secured, it seems like they lose interest. They become distant. They stop returning calls and ignore their companion. This leaves the other person feeling rejected and confused. The confusion happens because this transition can happen over night. The love that they felt before was so strong that the target cannot understand what happened. As the other person continues to try and revive the love, the narcissist rejects and hurts them even more. At some point they start to belittle and blame the other person in every way. Narcissists always scare the people they are involved with. The unfortunate target either becomes defensive or loses confidence in themselves.

The end of the relationship.

The end of the relationship is usually the most damaging to the other person. There are two ways a narcissistic relationship can end. Either the narcissist moves on to someone new, or the other person finds the strength to leave. Whatever happens, the target always wonders what went wrong and whether they were loved. The truth is that no, a real narcissist is not capable of love. Although the introductory phase of the relationship felt like love, it was only infatuation until boredom set in. In most cases, a narcissist will continue to return to their ex for help or reconciliation. They can easily convince their targets that they have changed and that it will be better this time. They rarely change, and it rarely gets better. They simply repeat the process of deep love, boredom, emotional abuse and abandonment.

While it is hard to realize someone is a narcissist, you can do it if you know the signs and behavioral patterns. With that knowledge they can be avoided. Avoidance is the best strategy, as true narcissists do not feel any of the emotions we may hope that they do. This means they rarely change, as they usually never feel the need to. A narcissistic relationship is a damaging one. These relationships last long enough to leave lasting negative feelings. A narcissist cannot have a meaningful relationship with anyone they meet. Their lack of empathy and vast amount of self-love will always leave them in need of new people to manipulate. They are usually fun, attractive and charming. This, however, wears off and their true, negative side quickly surfaces.

When You Find Yourself In A Relationship

With A Narcissist

Even though some people will try to refute it, there is a small part of narcissism in everyone. This is the reason why it is so difficult to know the extent to which someone is narcissistic unless you get to know them better. This is why it is so common to find people realizing that they are repulsed by the narcissistic tendencies of their partners yet they are the same ones, which attracted them in the first place. Therefore, even if you are in a romantic relationship with a narcissist, it does not necessarily mean that you can't love them. These people also have good traits such as great charisma, fun-loving attitude towards life and they are good at what they do. However, if the narcissist in your life brings you more heartbreak than joy, having the right strategies to defend yourself to make your relationship better or to minimize their manipulative nature is of utmost importance.

Consequently, if you are looking for ways on how to deal with the narcissist in your life, there are several strategies you can use.

Establish the type of narcissistic partner you are dealing with.

As you might have already figured out, most narcissists have low self-esteem. Unlike grandiose narcissists, vulnerable narcissists are introverted and you might not realize it when they begin getting in your way or start undercutting you. Thus, you need to determine which type of toxic partner you are in a romantic relationship with to be able to determine which approach to use when dealing with them.

Vulnerable narcissistic partner: He or she will be self-centered and self-absorbed to mask their inner core weakness.

Grandiose narcissistic partner: He or she will have a firm belief in their greatness — though at times they will actually be great.

Accept your annoyance.

If your narcissistic partner often becomes antagonistic and always gets under your skin, you need to accept your annoyance with their mannerisms in order to be able to find ways on how to best deal with them. This is because if you are always trying to outshine your toxic partner, chances are that you will only become more frustrated and annoyed with each passing day.

Appreciate the source of their behavior.

If you are in a romantic relationship with a narcissist, you should realize that your significant other will always try to undercut you and be sneaky as that is their nature. This means that they will question your authority in order to stir some mischief. By recognizing his/her insecurities, you will be able to provide the necessary reassurance to calm him/her down and get them to focus on the relevant matters at hand. However, you shouldn't give them too much reassurance, as this will fan their ego.

Evaluate the context.

Unlike popularly viewed, narcissism is not a get all or get nothing personality trait. Some events or occurrences will elicit greater insecurities than others. Thus, if you are in a romantic relationship with a narcissist, you should try not to praise someone else over and over again while with them. This is because it will only flare up their emotions, making them become vindictive, spiteful and defensively narcissistic. By evaluating the context of every situation, you should be able to know what and what not to do or say when in a romantic relationship with them.

Be positive.

If your partner usually derives pleasure from seeing others suffer, you shouldn't encourage their behavior. This means that whenever this happens, you shouldn't appear to be ruffled or even annoyed since with time, this behavior will diminish if he/she sees that you are not moved by their actions. In fact, by also following the other strategies along with this one, you will be able to ease the situation so that things can become better.

Avoid getting derailed.

Since your partner will at times try to take center stage and control what you do, you shouldn't give in to their demands. You should try and strike a balance between moving ahead in the direction you want and alleviating your toxic partner's insecurities and anxieties. However, if your partner is a grandiose narcissist, you may consider acknowledging their feelings and then moving on.

Have a good sense of humor.

In as much as calling your narcissistic partner's bluff may mean that you will ignore them, it also means that you will need to meet that bluff with a smile or laugh once in a while. Without being rude, you can simply point out their crude behavior with a joke. This is particularly essential if you have a grandiose type of toxic partner, as he/she will find it amusing and probably instructive.

Recognize their need for assistance.

If your significant other has a low self-esteem and has lots of feelings of inadequacy, you might need to seek professional intervention. This is because even those with long-standing behaviors can change with proper help. More so, tackling their issues yourself might not be feasible.

Regain or protect your independence.

Usually, narcissists tend to make you dependent on them. If you can, you should try and retain some of your independence, as this will make your toxic partner respect you. More so, it might even make him/her become dependent on you to some extent, for instance, if you take on the procurement responsibility.

Check on their willingness to change.

In as much as this might seem obvious, it is very crucial that you evaluate your partner carefully. You could, for instance, ask him/her if they are open to the idea of the both of you seeing a couple's therapist. If they agree, it will indicate that they are ready to change for the better and work on improving your romantic relationship.

Therefore, in as much as your narcissistic partner will at times upset or depress you, you should focus on applying correct strategies of dealing with them to make your romantic relationship balanced. This is because describing what you are going through to others might not give you the satisfaction you need. More so, your family members might not be inclined to believe you, when all they see is a charming partner. Consequently, by using the above strategies to deal with your toxic partner, you can be able to improve your relationship for the better, especially if you have children in the mix, whose well being is of utmost importance.

Chapter 12: Conditional Love

Love is simply a word to most mentally ill and the criminally insane. Love can never be fully understood conceptually. Most psychopaths will never know unconditional love, as they probably grew up in abusive homes where love was constantly withheld or nonexistent. A child that does not know unconditional love will not be emotionally aware of it when they are young.

Most people that have not experienced unconditional love will not ever be aware. Mental illness breeds mental illness like a vicious circle. If someone does not love you when you are misbehaving or are naughty, then they do not love you unconditionally.

Unconditional love is not loving the way you act or are behaving, as it is not liking your chosen behaviors, yet they will never abandon you in a time of need. Conditional love shows its form when the parent takes things away, crosses boundaries and privacy consistently, and has no trust in you.

There will be times that you misbehave, and something may be taken away to punish you, as this is not mean they are loving you conditionally. Conditional love will happen when the parent believes that you are offending or "misbehaving" even when you are not at fault or to blame. You will be the escape goat and blamed constantly.

You may be doing well in school and your parent still sifts and goes through your room looking for an excuse to punish you; these boundaries that are being crossed are not of a healthy nature. Children will make mistakes, as humans are flawed. Parents that show unconditional love will always love you, even if they do not love your behaviors or the decisions you make.

Deception and Intimidation is Second Nature

Playing the victim, fake tears, and emotional outbursts should not surprise you. Psychopaths, sociopaths, and the mentally insane can call upon tears as needed. Do not give in to the falsities of their so called realistic and genuine behaviors.

From an early age psychopaths and sociopaths practice making faces in the mirror, that typically come naturally to prosocial people. It is not unheard of for psychopaths to work on their smiles, practice kissing, or generate tears on command. Deception is an innate part of who they are.

Imagine someone that does not feel much emotion. They have anger and boredom mostly, but do not grasp much more than that. Psychopath's hate being bored more than anything, as they will amuse themselves by practicing constantly their masks of deception.

Manipulation and deception appear to be very natural and comforting to psychopaths. Sociopath's can be used interchangeably because they are psychopath's too. Deception will be their main defense next to intimidation.

Intimidation can take many forms and isn't always an out right verbal threat. Passive aggression is a huge part of a psychopath's demeanor. They will tend to openly avoid confrontation but will not forget or let anything go. They will remember for long periods of time and not get upset, yet they will exact revenge when it is the perfect moment to execute.

Intimidation can be passive aggressive stares or insidious looks like when a mom catches you doing something you're not supposed to. These looks are no ordinary looks, they are "death" stares or down right bone-chilling evil looks.

Playing the victim will sound like a threat. "I don't know what I'll do without you," as they threaten their own life to get control over you. They will say things like, "nobody helps" or "nobody lies me." They will play the victim card to enable them to continually reinforce their negative behaviors.

If you give in to their pleas or manipulation, then you will be feeling guilt over someone else's behaviors; it is the predicament because you are breeding irrational guilt. Irrational guilt will encourage continuous manipulation in your relationship. Initially, you may think you can handle or ignore these behaviors;

however, over time you will be effective greatly, just one small piece at a time.

Chapter 13: Cause, Inspiration, And Relationships

I have been showing a lot lately on sociopathy as a function of talking about tv about Jodi Arias, the woman tried for the 2008 murder of her sweetheart. I've come to ask myself some very basic questions about those who are sociopaths, as I very much expect that Ms. Arias certifies as one. Further, just recently reading previous Harvard professor Martha Stout's book, The Sociopath Next Door, I've been reminded how mysterious sociopathy remains.

Part of what makes sociopathy so fascinating is that we understand very little about what causes it. The sociopath overall is little understood, manifested primarily in the conventional belief that the sociopath has the harmful intent to hurt others. The truth, however, is more complicated than a single answer permits. Are sociopaths bad people? It's simple to utter a full-throated "Yes!" for so many reasons, but the reality is that sociopaths do not always have malicious emotions toward others. The problem is that they have really little true feeling at all for others, which allows them to treat others as items. The influence of their conduct is certainly malicious, though the intent isn't necessarily the same thing.

Ultimately, the sociopath normally mentally destroys the ones that are close to him or her, but the sociopath ruins them in a way consistent with their special method to others: They take them out like your typical person kills off characters in a computer game. Those in the wake of the sociopath suffer because they have the liability sociopaths don't-- real human emotions that come from a deep sense of social commitments to others, an ethical anchor that's supposed to be part and parcel of having relationships.

The sense of entitlement that includes sociopathy is amazing to the ones who comply with the social laws and conventions of our culture. Where does the entitlement originated from? It originates from an underlying sense of rage. Sociopaths feel deeply mad and resentful underneath their often-charming outside, and this rage fuels their sense that they have the actual right to act out in whichever way they happen to choose at the time. Everything is up for grabs with sociopaths and absolutely nothing is off limits.

In relationships, sociopaths are the epitome of Machiavellian creatures. If they were astrological signs, they would be Geminis, with 2 distinct 'selfs' at work. They are duplicity incarnate, with a refined self revealed to the world and a hidden, hidden self that has a rigid and determining agenda: Assume the greatest level of the social hierarchy and win, win, win. It's often the kindest and most trusting individuals who suffer the most at the hands of sociopaths, and the healing process for these individuals continues long after the relationship has ended. Those in the wake of the sociopath are usually left just wondering, What happened to me? Why does this one person have such a powerful effect on me?

In the media, I am often asked what triggers sociopathy. One of the most often asked questions is: "Are they born this way?" The truth is that we do not know. Stout (2005) summarize the research well, explaining that as much as 50 percent of the reason for sociopathy can be credited to heritability, while the remaining percentage is a complicated and not-yet-understood mix of ecological aspects. (Especially, a history of youth abuse amongst sociopaths isn't always present.) Similarly, Ferguson (2010) performed a meta-analysis and learned that 56 percent of the difference in Antisocial Personality Disorder, the official disorder of sociopathy, can be clarified through hereditary influences.

I'm impressed to say that I have large tanks of empathy for the sociopath. At the same time, to see the life trajectory of a sociopath, it's hard to not feel sad that the sociopath has a presence that separates him from the large bulk of 'typical' people. They typically end up in jail and never ever truly know what it feels a lot like to really love and trust. Just imagine what that existence is a lot like, not just for a week or month or summer season, but for life. Do they even know what they're missing? No, but they live in a constant state of hypervigilance, seeing the world in a sterile, game-like way. They have no real attachment to anybody.

Given the significant role biology appears to play in creating or planting the seed of sociopathy, are sociopaths deserving of some empathy? If, as the research suggests, sociopaths are born with a predisposition to sociopathy, it means that they don't have overall control over their conduct. To think that a poor kid is born with such a horrific, life-long liability is an awfully miserable reality. After all, no child deserves to carry around that sort of luggage.

I found something online about a British model who was the victim of a horrific crime in which a man threw acid on her face as she walked on the walkway of a crowded city street. At the time, many individuals responded to the news in the media and called the criminal "evil." My handle the topic was that evil wasn't an adequate term for the man who did the criminal offense, favoring instead the idea that the lawbreaker was mentally ill. Actually, as a psychologist, I don't really believe true evil exists. Instead, I see this circumstance-- and the larger issue of sociopathy-- as a source of malfunctioning, as though a robotic gone wild. We can try to call it whatever we wish, but the truth remains that we don't completely comprehend it and, unless brain research shows otherwise with time, we could never totally understand the etiological process underlying sociopathy.

The present Jodi Arias trial has brought the psychological maze of sociopathy back into American culture, a trend that emerges each few years when a legal case has all the mendings for a super-sized marvelous trial. Day after day, Ms. Arias beings in the courtroom, affectless, as if a character in a movie rather than her own life. While my sense is that Ms. Arias is a true sociopath, to see her every day in the courtroom is to see a woman who appears incredibly lost, lonesome, and emotionless. In so many ways, she seems to be the perfect face of sociopathy: ever-changing, highly protected, and empty. At the end of the day, she is an effective pointer of how complicated, hazardous and, yes, misinterpreted the sociopath remains today.

Chapter 14: The Importance Of Accountability

I think we have established that disrespect and intimidation are not good foundations for a relationship, and that there needs to be a balance between the parties because without balance we might be talking of a relationship where one believes he or she owns the other person (power and control, which are the main traits of imbalanced relationships), and we should be aware that people cannot own people nowadays, which would be called slavery and it is illegal in this part of the world.

We've also covered love and the dangers of not receiving love, from ourselves and others.

Now, let's talk about Accountability, or the power to take responsibility for our own actions, with or without consequences.

Truth be told, being liable for something and actually paying for it doesn't necessarily go together in real life, so for the sake of keeping focus we'll just talk about taking responsibility leaving out the rest, as it is irrelevant to this point.

What is relevant is that taking responsibility for our own actions is a sign of maturity, and an excellent virtue.

That is without making excuses, simply accepting that we made a mistake, or a bad judgment call, and that we are not infallible, which by the way also shows that we do not have a god complex.

All in all, it is an important personality trait.

In relationships, it also keeps the balance, so it is in fact a lot more important than people give it credit for.

But how does Accountability keep balance in the relationship, you might wonder.

Well, think about it this way: If one of you is never at fault, this person won't ever feel the necessity to do anything for it.

Now you can see what I'm getting at?

Let me rephrase this. The problem with not taking responsibility is that things may get broken, but not necessarily fixed, which in the best of cases becomes extremely annoying, and in the long term, dysfunctional.

Imagine having to deal with someone who brings problems to you but that rather leave you upset and angry dealing with them, than do anything about it. Then it is not so much about just breaking things anymore, it is about dropping them on you, and then letting you down too:

For not taking their part of the responsibility.

For not feeling that they need to do something about it.

For leaving you alone to deal with it.

This is not your mess, why do you have to deal with it when they don't?

That last one is the real deal,

Why do you have to deal with it when they don't.

You see? People say that accountability shows maturity because when a child is in trouble, he or she will take this problem to their parents (or trusted adults) to solve. That is what children do.

Adults on the other hand, are expected to take control and sort it.

So if the adult takes no responsibility, and does not feel like he or she should be sorting anything, what happens with the issue? It doesn't magically disappear. It stays unresolved OR it gets dumped on to someone else.

Living with someone unaccountable is exhausting.

It's like adopting an adult that will not learn and will not leave the home, ever.

It's living with constant problems created for you and laid at your door.

It's sharing your life with a machine that systematically breaks things, but does not see the need to fix them.

It's constantly being blamed for association.

There can never be a balance in the relationship if one of you is unaccountable. All the weight will be dumped on the other one's shoulders.

So, are you living with someone or carrying their issues?

Narcissistic Tendencies

The worst example of unaccountability is Narcissism, because the narcissist has a sense of entitlement where he or she cannot accept blame for anything, no matter how selfish or harmful this is for others.

Have you ever seen this poem?

A Narcissist's Prayer:

'That didn't happen.

And if it did, it wasn't that bad.

And if it was, that's not a big deal.

And if it is, that's not my fault.

And if it was, I didn't mean it.

And if I did

You deserved it.'

— Author Unknown.

It is a great description of the attitude of a narcissist against accountability.

And thinking about it, it looks like an incredible amount of work to avoid responsibility too; no wonder narcissists are known for irritability and mood swings, they must be exhausted all the time!

Let's go through the whole process to see how much work they put into unaccountability.

First they deny what you are saying, which must take at least a bit of time because you obviously are not going to just drop it if the person in front of you, who should be apologising right now, is basically either calling you a liar or trying to convince you that you see things that are not real. It will definitely take them some time and effort to engage you on that line of thought.

Then, when they have no other option but to admit that it happened, they change tactics and move on to dismissing it. That's another argument in itself.

When that doesn't work, they try to convince you that it didn't really matter that much, dismissing that it did matter to you, and throwing in more time and effort, and more arguments.

Then, when that didn't go away, because even if it wasn't that big a deal to start with, all the arguing actually made it much much bigger, now they bluntly refuse to be accountable for it.

At this point they will try to convince you that they didn't know what they were doing (?!), dodging again responsibility, and when that doesn't go down well, they simply justify themselves with any excuse they can think of...

Ultimately blaming you for it.

Just by explaining this process, I am exhausted. It has to be A LOT of work to actually do it to someone. And it is very mean, so they really must loath that person to put them through all that: This is not a love expression, this is plain nasty.

As opposed to normal behaviour which could simply entail a "My bad, luv", maybe followed by a meaningful hug or even an offer to fix or replace what's broken.

Obviously, if what's broken is a bone in an argument, don't stay to ask for accountability, go. Go now. In this case accountability would be the least of your worries, and your safety should be your priority. Don't argue with a violent person, just leave as soon as you can, and don't look back.

But going back to our poem, remember that narcissism is a very specific behavioural pattern, very extreme and very harmful psychologically, so if you have identified that pattern, you need to understand that you are dealing with something that you cannot fix, and you cannot make better.

This is really really important for you to understand:

There is absolutely nothing that you can possibly do that will improve your relationship with a narcissist.

And this is because the relationship is not up to you alone, no matter how much your partner insists on putting the weight of it on your shoulders.

Think about it: The word Relationship in itself implies that there is more than one individual involved in it. So how come it would be exclusively up to you to take responsibility for it? Who appointed you? I can only imagine.

However, in reality, a romantic relationship is intrinsically a thing of (at least, and normally) two people, where these two need to take responsibility for it. In a manner of speech, it's a two way road, where you give and you receive, and you both break and you both fix.

One alone can't do it, because, as we said before, imagine the mess if two people are breaking things, but only one is fixing them. Thus if one of you does not show the capability to take responsibility, and is ultimately blaming you for whatever it is that caused the problem in the first place, it's time for you to cut your losses and leave.

And let me stretch at this point that everybody has the capability for taking responsibility, they might just choose not to use it.

In other words, as adults they technically could. Which is why I said show capability as opposed to have capability.

And as we have seen, it is a lot more work to avoid responsibility than to take it, so no normal adult would choose that path, right? You would have to be crazy.

Unaccountability in General

Anyway, not all individuals who avoid responsibility become narcissists (only the very special ones), and I had the unusual opportunity of getting involved in relationships of both cases, lucky me.

My relationship with the narcissist gradually became a definition of hell on earth. He almost completely destroyed me emotionally as well as psychologically. It took me around 7 years with this person to realise that I needed to get out or I would end up killing myself, and an extra 7 or so to get the courage to join the local domestic violence support group, because he successfully convinced me that what he was doing to me "wasn't really abuse", that it was "all in my head", and then when I left him, he put me through even more hell, claiming that "I made him do it", that it was "not his fault", and finally declaring that "I deserve it".

It truly was as if he had copied the Narcissist's Prayer text, and put it into action word by word.

Unfortunately, because of all the headwork he put me through to minimise and dismiss what was happening, and a natural disposition we all humans have to believe that 'he can't have done that on purpose, it has to be a mistake', it took me a very long time to realise that I needed to leave.

But it was his persistence on not taking responsibilities what triggered me thinking that something was utterly wrong. His turning things around to dodge the blame for anything and everything, without fail, was the beginning of my wakening, because nobody is that blameless.

Think about it.

Then many years later, I was in a relationship with a different man who was younger than me, and my first reaction to his lack of understanding of what accountability stands for was that perhaps he was simply immature. But watching my child taking responsibility for having eaten sweets before dinner and without permission, or misplacing her school lanyard, I realised that I was wrong about him.

If a kid understands accountability, his attitude couldn't be about immaturity, it had to be plain neglect.

He didn't take responsibility because he didn't want it. And so he would do all sorts of things that he shouldn't, and not do any of the stuff that he should have done, only to justify himself by blaming the world, the circumstances, his bad luck, or simply denying that he was ultimately responsible for any of it.

He did anything he could to avoid responsibility for his actions, which came at a great cost to me, because by not taking responsibility he was giving himself a green card to continue the wrong doing.

Which he did, of course, we are who we are after all.

That is the importance of accountability. It is the difference between:

I break something, so I fix it.

And

I break something, and I blame you, so I don't have to fix anything.

You see the different dynamics? Number two is truly a number two in the relationship.

Moral of the story: You can't have a balanced relationship with someone who does not take responsibility for his or her own actions. It is not possible.

And as we have said many times over, without balance...

You do the maths.

Chapter 15: Dealing With A Sociopath

Normal people possess a natural affinity for other individuals. This is why it is impossible to hurt someone without feeling at least the slightest pinch of guilt or remorse. Normal human beings naturally care for their fellow human beings. That's because we share the feelings of fear, anguish, suffering, and frustration.

There are times when we hurt the ones we love, although we do not mean to. In this case, the guilt is worse, because in addition to causing them pain, the remorse is heightened due to our affection for them. Our attachment with them makes the guilt over hurting them much worse. With a sociopath, such natural feelings of attachment and affection are non-existent, as are guilt, conscience, and empathy.

Sociopaths are more common than you think.
According to research, sociopaths comprise about four percent of the population. This goes to say that sociopaths are quite common. They are everywhere, and most of them are not so easy to detect. In fact, people who come into contact with sociopaths are in denial. They simply cannot admit that someone they thought they knew, someone they have trusted, is actually a sociopath incapable of love.

It is not easy to identify a sociopath. This is mainly because they are clever in building up their cover. But, there are a few questions that may lead you to clues that can help you detect a sociopath. The trouble here is that it may prove difficult to be objective in your assessment, especially when this person is someone close to you. In any case, you can ask yourself the following questions to help you compare this person with others in your life and ultimately find out whether he or she is a sociopath or not.

•Does it feel like this person is only using you?
•Does it feel like this person does not really care about you?
•Does this person lie to you constantly?
•Does this person contradict his own statements or stories?
•Does this person take from you and never seem to have the intention of giving back?
•Does this person use pity? Does he make you feel sorry for him too often?
•Does this person make you feel guilty or turn the tables and make it appear like you are at fault?
•Does it feel like this person is taking

advantage of your kindness?
•Does this person get easily bored? Does he seek constant stimulation?

•Does he often use flattery to get to your good side?
•Does this person make you feel worried?
•Does this person make you feel like he is entitled or like you owe him?
•Does this person tend to blame others for his mistakes? Does he refuse to acknowledge his own faults and take the blame?
Finally, does this person seem to do such things more than any other people in your life? If most of your answers are affirmative, then there is a good chance that you are indeed dealing with a sociopath. Even if he is not one, this person is clearly not good for you.

Dealing with a sociopath is not easy. Whether you are in a romantic or business

175

relationship with this person, there are a few rules you must follow. Doing these things can help minimize the damage and the possible harm that may come your way.

Seek immediate help from a professional. Unless you make an effort first to understand how a sociopath operates, you have a minimal chance of surviving a sociopath. A professional can help you learn the motivations and the tactics of a sociopath. A professional can help you understand that this person is different, not to mention the fact that they are very good at mind control.

Someone who specializes in sociopathy can help you understand how you have been trapped in a vicious cycle of deception and manipulation, and how it can be stopped. Finally, you can see through the illusion that the sociopath in your life has created. You will realize what the relationship is all about. In this way, you can stop this person from controlling you.

The moment you become aware of the sociopath's true identity is the same moment he starts to lose control and power over you. He may still try to, but the effects become minimal.

Stop making contact.

As long as you give the sociopath a chance, he will continue to make attempts to manipulate you. This makes it much wiser to stop contact completely. That means you should not call him, receive his calls, answer his emails, or even read his messages.

There is no hope of reasoning with a sociopath. Such a person is incapable of feeling the same emotions as normal people do. This person will feel no guilt for what he has put you through.

Do not try to give the sociopath any ultimatums. It will never work. You are bound to lose. The sociopath's advantage is his lack of guilt. So, do not waste any more energy trying to make peace with this person.

Once you make the attempt to flee from the sociopath, you must also inform the people around you about the situation. The tendency is for the sociopath to contact them and get on their good side. The sociopath is more likely to isolate you from the people you care about and to make it appear like you are the one with the big issue. You must stop it before it happens.

Do not share any more information. After a while of being with the sociopath, he has more likely learned some information about you, your family, your work, and your friends. This information will be used and may have already been used against you. Remind yourself that you are dealing with a professional manipulator. Do not give him the chance to use any more information to take control of you.

Understand both your strengths and weaknesses.

Before leading you into his world, the sociopath has taken his time to learn about and understand your strengths and weaknesses. And, he has used this knowledge well. By understanding your strengths, and especially your weaknesses, you become more able to recognize the instances when the sociopath will make an attempt to press these buttons.

Stick to your instincts. You may have seen the signs, but you may have given this person the benefit of the doubt. A sociopath is not worthy of such a benefit. You become subject to further manipulation and you are repeatedly dragged into the worst of situations when you continue to override your instincts.

Do not make any attempts at reformation. It is important to understand that a sociopath does not think there is anything wrong with him. Treatment for sociopaths, especially for adults, is more often than not, useless. In fact, treatment may make them even worse than they already are.

Just like drugs can be misused, therapy can also be misused. Sociopaths abuse the privilege of therapy to get more information about people's behavior. You can trust that such information will be used for their advantage later.

You must accept the fact that a sociopath cannot change his very nature. In fact, sociopaths do not even recognize the need for change.

Realize none of it is your fault. You have been tricked. That is the plain truth. This person has appealed to your good nature and has used you. If you continue to let him, he will drain you up. It is also important to realize and understand that none of this is your fault.

You should not blame yourself. So, be forgiving of yourself. Of course, the story changes when the sociopath turns out to be someone who is part of your family. You are bound by blood and obligation. That means it is not an option to walk away. This does not mean, however, that you should let your guard down. Take the same precautions. Keep informed and seek help for you and your loved one.

Conclusion

Dealing with sociopaths is never easy. Being devoid of conscience and empathy, sociopaths may indeed pose extreme threat and danger to the lives of ordinary people around them. They could hurt others emotionally, psychologically, or even physically without feeling the least bit shameful or remorseful about their deed.

Having a sociopath in your life is a serious matter. Anyone is indeed very much vulnerable to their deceit, manipulation, and abuse. However, this does not always mean that it is something which is impossible to avoid. There is definitely something you can do to protect yourself. And the first step towards doing so may be to be fully-informed about the sociopaths that may just be so freely mingling with ordinary individuals in society.

www.ingramcontent.com/pod-product-compliance
Lightning Source LLC
Chambersburg PA
CBHW060334030426
42336CB00011B/1331